Railroad Collectibles
An Illustrated Value Guide

3rd Edition

Stanley L. Baker

COLLECTOR BOOKS
A Division of Schroeder Publishing Co., Inc.

The current values in this book should be used only as a guide. They are not intended to set prices, which vary from one section of the country to another. Auction prices as well as dealer prices vary greatly and are affected by condition as well as demand. Neither the Author nor the Publisher assumes responsibility for any losses that might be incurred as a result of consulting this guide.

Additional copies of this book may be ordered from:

COLLECTOR BOOKS
P.O. Box 3009
Paducah, Kentucky 42001

@$17.95 Add $1.00 for postage and handling.

Copyright: Stanley Baker, 1985
ISBN: 0-89145-171-4

TABLE OF CONTENTS

INTRODUCTION

This Third Edition of *Railroad Collectibles* (the first edition, published by Hawthorn was titled *The Railroadiana Collector's Price Guide*) finds all reports indicating that prices are continuing to rise as this hobby continues to gain in popularity. Collecting railroadiana, which has been going on for many years, but which did not really come into its own until the Iron Horse breathed its last and passenger trains came to the end of the line, has now proliferated until it has become a securely established hobby all across the country. Both collectors and dealers need to be aware of the many collectibles in this field and their current value.

All prices shown are retail, reflecting the current market as of this writing. Dealers buying for re-sale pay less, depending upon their mark-up. Prices have been arrived at by studying those realized at antique shows and shops, railroadiana meets and sales, ads found in the antique trade journals, through the various mail order lists, and among collectors in the field. Auction prices, also incorporated in the Guide, often have great variation. Also bear in mind that prices often vary in different locations of the country.

It cannot be emphasized enough that condition plays a very important role in pricing, and you will note this fact repeated over and over again throughout the Guide. Also, pieces with a railroad marking from a long-gone, defunct railroad carry a much higher price tag. Needless to say, supply and demand is the rule governing all pricing, as sometimes a passionate collector is willing to pay far more than the current market price for a certain item especially needed to round out his collection. And, of course, there is always the chance of paying far less, should you be lucky enough to come across a "real" bargain!

As with all antiques, top dollar is paid for rarities, such as a choice piece of dining car china. For instance, the complete set of Illinois Central Railroad's beautiful "French Quarter" service plates brings big money at auction. We all realize that there are too many variables for any price to be firm, as it is very difficult to set a value on a piece of rare railroadiana. All prices listed should be used as a GUIDE, and not final authority.

The same general format has been followed as in previous Editions, with a short narrative at the beginning of each of the 45 listings, summarizing the category in as few words as possible in an effort to make the Guide easy to use as a handy, take-along reference book. The attempt has been made to cover each category with as representative a grouping of items as possible. No new categories have been added, but a number of the headings include additional listings pertinent to that particular category. It goes without saying that any attempt at completeness is impossible, as collectors will always come up with things I had no idea existed. This is one of the fascinations of collecting railroadiana - discoveries are being made all the time.

Railroadiana is basically divided into two main categories, paper and hardware, with a vast quantity of items in each. It is open to question which is the more popular; it is largely a matter of personal preference. Discriminating can make you an expert in your thing, while generalizing provides you with a broader scope of the hobby as a whole. Many collectors do both - have a varied collection to which they are continually adding, while at the same time specializing in one particular category. Searching for railroadiana, however you collect, requires perseverance. Collectors should get to know as much as possible about railroad artifacts in order to make their own evaluation and be able to recognize a good piece. Many items are unique, one of a kind, and their value must be judged subjectively.

Where is railroadiana to be found? Railroad collectibles are being sold through lists sent out by mail-order dealers, or through the classified ads in various railroad or hobby magazines and general antique publications. Local antique shops are good sources, also the large antique shows across the country. The retired railroad employee is another source, for many of these men kept their caps and badges, locks and keys, lanterns, ticket punches, and so on. If they were not disposed of during the owner's lifetime, the estate sale is often a good source, as are the garage sales, flea markets and auctions. Collectors also do a lot of buying selling and trading among themselves. Surplus stocks of switch-stand and other lamps and their accessories are sometimes available from railroad supply companies. Oil cans and other tinware can quite often be obtained from manufacturers in this line. There are other such sources, as railroad museums, where the collector can obtain railroadiana today.

Good luck in your search!

All photos by the author.

Note: An asterisk has been placed after each item illustrated in the Guide.

KEY TO RAILROAD ABBREVIATIONS

INITIALS	RAILROAD NAME	ALSO KNOWN AS
AA	Ann Arbor RR	
A&GW	Atlantic & Great Western RR	
A&S	Alton & Southern RR	
A ST	Atlanta Street RR	
A&StL	Atlantic & St. Lawrence RR	
AC&S	Atlantic City and Shore RR	
ACL	Atlantic Coast Line RR	Sea Level Route
AT&SF	Atchison Topeka & Santa Fe Ry	Santa Fe
B&A	Boston & Albany RR	
B&F	Boston & Fitchburg RR	
B&MR RR	Burlington & Missouri River RR	
B&Me	Boston & Maine RR	Line of The Minute Man
B&O	Baltimore & Ohio RR	
BAR	Bangor & Aroostook RR	
BCER	British Columbia Electric Ry	
BCR&M	Burlington Cedar Rapids & Minnesota RR	
BCR&N	Burlington Cedar Rapids & Northern Ry	The Iowa Route
BN	Burlington Northern	
BO&SW	Baltimore Ohio & Southwestern Ry	
BR&P	Buffalo Rochester & Pittsburgh RR	
C&A	Chicago & Alton RR	Alton The Only Way
C&EI	Chicago & Eastern Illinois RR	The Noiseless Route
C&G	Columbus & Greenville Ry	
C&NW	Chicago & Northwestern Ry	Northwestern Line
C&O	Chesapeake & Ohio Ry	
C&S	Colorado & Southern Ry	
C&WI	Chicago & Western Indiana RR	
C&WM	Chicago & West Michigan RR	
CB&Q	Chicago Burlington & Quincy RR	Burlington Route
CC&L	Chicago Cincinnati & Louisville Ry	
CCC	Cape Cod Central RR	
CCC&StL	Cleveland Cincinnati Chicago & St. Louis Ry	Big Four Route
CGW	Chicago Great Western Ry	The Corn Belt Route The Maple Leaf Route
CI&L	Chicago Inidianapolis & Louisville RR	Monon Route
CK&N	Chicago Kansas & Nebraska Ry	
CM	Colorado Midland	Midland Route
CI&W	Cincinnati Indiana & Western Ry	
CM&PS	Chicago Milwaukee & Puget Sound RR	
CM&StP	Chicago Milwaukee & St. Paul Ry	Milwaukee Road
CMStP&P	Chicago Milwaukee St. Paul & Pacific RR	Milwaukee Road
CNJ	Central RR Co of New Jersey	
CNR	Canadian National Ry	
CNS&M	Chicago North Shore & Milwaukee RR	The North Shore Line
CO&G	Chocktaw Oklahoma & Gulf RR	

INITIALS	RAILROAD NAME	ALSO KNOWN AS
CPR	Canadian Pacific Ry	
CRI&P	Chicago Rock Island & Pacific RR	Rock Island
CStP&KC	Chicago St. Paul & Kansas City Ry	
CStPM&O	Chicago St. Paul Mpls. & Omaha Ry	Omaha
CStPM&DM	Chicago St. Paul Mpls. & Des Moines	
CV	Central Vermont Ry	
CW&B	Cincinnati Washington & Baltimore RR	
D&H	Delaware & Hudson RR	
D&IR	Duluth & Iron Range RR	Vermillion Route
D&RGW	Denver & Rio Grand Western RR	Rio Grande
D&RG	Denver & Rio Grande RR	Rio Grande
D&SF	Denver & Santa Fe Ry	
D&SL	Denver & Salt Lake RR	The Moffat Road
DL&W	Delaware Lackawanna & Western RR	Lackawanna
DM&IR	Duluth Missabe & Iron Range Ry	
DM&N	Duluth Missabe & Northern Ry	
DM&V	Delaware Maryland & Virginia RR	
DP	Minneapolis, St. Paul, Rochester & Dubuque Electric Traction Co.	Dan Patch
DSS&A	Duluth South Shore & Atlantic Ry	The South Shore
E&TH	Evansville & Terre Haute Ry	
EJ&E	Elgin Joliet & Eastern Ry	Chicago Outer Belt Line
EL	Erie Lackawanna RR	
ERR	Erie RR	Erie
F&NE	Fairchild & Northeastern Ry	
F&PM	Flint & Pere Marquette RR	
FDDM&S	Fort Dodge Des Moines & Southern RR	
FE&MV	Fremont Elkhorn & Missouri Valley RR	
FEC	Florida East Coast Ry	Flagler System
FJ&G	Fonda Johnstown & Gloversville RR	
FRR	Fitchburg RR	The Hoosiac Tunnel Route
FW&DC	Fort Worth & Denver City Ry	
GB&W	Green Bay & Western RR	Green Bay Route
GC&SF	Gulf Colorado & Santa Fe Ry	
GF&A	Gulf Florida & Alabama Ry	
GH&S	Gulf Houston & Southern Ry	
GM&N	Gulf Mobile & Northern RR	
GM&O	Gulf Mobile & Ohio RR	The Alton Route
GN	Great Northern Ry	
GRR	Grand Rapids Railway Co.	
GS&F	Georgia Southern & Florida Ry	
GTP	Grand Trunk Pacific Ry	
GTR	Grand Trunk Ry System	
GTW	Grand Trunk Western RR	
H&BT	Huntingdon & Broad Top RR	
H&NH	Hartford & New Haven RR	
HBL	Harbor Belt Line RR	
H&TC	Houston & Texas Central RR	
IC	Illinois Central RR	Mississippi Valley Route
ICStRY	Illinois Central Street Railway Co.	
IHB	Indiana Harbor Belt RR	
IR	Indiana Railroad System	
IRT	Interborough Rapid Transit Co. N.Y.	
IStRy	Indianapolis Street Railway Co.	

INITIALS	RAILROAD NAME	ALSO KNOWN AS
JC	Jersey Central RR	
K&IT	Kentucky & Indiana Terminal Ry	
KCM&B	Kansas City Memphis & Birmingham RR	
KCP&G	Kansas City Pittsburgh & Gulf RR	
KCS	Kansas City Southern Ry	Straight as The Crow Flies
KCStJ&CB	Kansas City St. Jo. & Council Bluffs RR	
KCT	Kansas City Terminal Ry Co.	
L&N	Louisville & Nashville RR	
L&NE	Lehigh & New England RR	
LI	Long Island RR	
LS&MS	Lake Shore & Michigan Southern Ry	The Fast Mail Line
LV	Lehigh Valley RR	
MEX. NAT.	Mexican National RR	
M&I	Minnesota & International Ry	
M&NW	Minnesota & Northwestern RR	
M&O	Mobile & Ohio RR	
M&PP	Manitou & Pike's Peak Ry	The Cog Wheel Route
M&S	Milwaukee & Superior RR	
M&StL	Minneapolis & St. Louis Ry	The Peoria Gateway The Albert Lea Route
M&StP	Milwaukee & St. Paul Ry	
MC	Michigan Central RR	Niagara Falls Route
MEC	Maine Central RR	
ME	Minneapolis Eastern Ry	
MHC&W	Mississippi Hill City & Western RR	
MKT	Missouri Kansas Texas RR	Katy
MN&S	Minneapolis Northfield & Southern Ry	
MP	Missouri Pacific RR	Mo-Pac
MRR	Manistee RR	
MS&NI	Michigan Southern & Northern Indiana Ry	
MSO	Missabe Southern RR	
MStP&A	Minneapolis St. Paul & Ashland Ry	
MStP&SSM	Minneapolis St. Paul & Sault Ste. Marie Ry	Soo Line
MT RY	Minnesota Transfer	
NAT.RYS. MEX	National Railways of Mexico	
N&W	Norfolk & Western Ry	
NC	North Carolina RR	
NC&StL	Nashville Chattanooga & St. Louis Ry	The Dixie Line
NI	Northern Indiana Ry	
NJC	New Jersey Central	Jersey Central Lines
NKP	New York Chicago & St. Louis RR	Nickel Plate Road
NP	Northern Pacific Ry	Yellowstone Park Line
NWP	Northwestern Pacific RR	
NYB&M	New York Boston & Montreal RR	
NYC	New York Central RR	
NYC&HR	New York Central & Hudson River RR	
NY&NH	New York & New Haven RR	
NYNH&H	New York New Haven & Hartford RR	New Haven
NYC&StL	New York Chicago & St. Louis RR	Nickel Plate
NYLE&W	New York Lake Erie & Western	
NYO&W	New York Ontario & Western Ry	O&W, OW
NY&E	New York & Erie RR	
NYP&B	New York Providence & Boston RR	

INITIALS	RAILROAD NAME	ALSO KNOWN AS
OR&N	Oregon Railroad & Navigation Co.	
OSL	Oregon Short Line RR	
OVE	Ohio Valley Electric RR	
P&LE	Pittsburgh & Lake Erie RR	
P&O	Portland & Ogdensburgh RR	
P&PU	Peoria & Pekin Union Ry	
P&R	Philadelphia & Reading Ry	Reading
PC	Penn Central RR	
PE	Pacific Electric Ry	
PM	Pere Marquette RR	
POD	Post Office Department	
PPC CO	Pullman Palace Car Co.	
PRR	Pennsylvania RR	Pennsy, Penna
PTRA	Port Terminal Railroad Assn.	
PORT.	Portland RR	
PW&B	Philadelphia Wilmington & Baltimore RR	
QA&P	Quanah Acme & Pacific Ry	Quanah Route
R&I Ry	Rockford & Interurban Ry	
REA	Railway Express Agency	Ry. Ex. Agy.; Am.Ry.Ex.
RDG	Reading Ry	
RF&P	Richmond Fredericksburg & Potomac RR	
RI	Rock Island Lines	
RRI&StL	Rockford Rock Island & St. Louis RR	
RUT	Rutland RR	Green Mountain Line
SAL	Seaboard Air Line Ry	Seaboard
SCL	Seaboard Coast Line RR	Seaboard
SD&A	San Diego & Arizona Ry	
SM	Southern Minnesota RR	
SP	Southern Pacific Co.	Sunset Route
SP&S	Spokane Portland & Seattle Ry	
SR	Southern Ry	
StJ	St. Joe Ry	
StL&SF	St. Louis & San Francisco Ry	Frisco Lines
StL&SW	St. Louis & South Western Ry	Cotton Belt Route
StLIM&S	St. Louis Iron Mountain & Southern Ry	Iron Mountain Route
StL&OR	St. Louis & Ohio River RR	
StP&D	St. Paul & Duluth RR	
StP&P	St. Paul & Pacific RR	
StP&SC	St. Paul & Sioux City RR	
StPCyRy	St. Paul City Railway	
StPM&M	St. Paul Minneapolis & Manitoba Ry	
StPUD	St. Paul Union Depot	
StPUSY	St. Paul Union Stock Yards Co.	
SURYs	State University Railways (NC)	
T RY	Toronto Ry	
T&P	Texas & Pacific RR	Sunshine Special Route
T&YR	Toronto & York Radial Ry	
TC	Texas Central RR	The Lone Star Route
TP&W	Toledo Peoria & Western Ry	
TRRA	Terminal Railroad Assn.	
TStL&KC	Toledo St. Louis & Kansas City RR	
UP	Union Pacific RR	The Overland Route
USTVA	United States Tennessee Valley Authority	
UTC OF IND.	United Transit Co. of Indiana	

INITIALS	RAILROAD NAME	ALSO KNOWN AS
USY OF O	Union Stock Yards of Omaha	
V RR	Valley RR	
VGN	Virginian Ry	
VL	Vandalia Line	
W&LE	Wheeling & Lake Erie Ry	
W&StP	Winona & St. Peter RR	
WAB	Wabash RR	The Banner Route
W RY	Wheeling Ry	
WC	Wisconsin Central RR	
WCStRR	West Chicago Street Ry Co.	
WM	Western Maryland Ry	
WP	Western Pacific RR	Feather River Route
WP&YR	White Pass & Yukon Route	
WStL&P	Wabash St. Louis & Pacific Ry	
Y&MV	Yazoo & Mississippi Valley RR	

ADVERTISING SOUVENIRS

Thousands of advertising souvenir items, such as paperweights, spoons, fans, letter openers, pocket mirrors, match boxes, and novelty items of all kinds were widely distributed by the railroads down through the years. Earlier pieces are bringing high prices, and those from the later years are priced according to their scarcity and demand. The rare and unique items usually go at auction.

BCR&N: Coin type paperweight, 2¾" dia., "Albert Lea Route" 1890s 50.00
BURLINGTON: Paperweight, First Vista Dome car on base, 1945, silver finish 75.00*
BURLINGTON: Stainless steel match case, Zephyrus emblem, 1934 . . . . .25.00

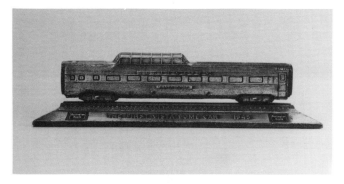

Mini-model desk piece

CANADIAN NATIONAL: Bottle opener, steel, 3¾" long, flat type 7.50
CGW: Pocket knife, red diesel frt. train on pearlized handle, 1950s 25.00
CGW: Round metal paperweight, 2¾", maple leaf emblem on celluloid covering, 1890s 50.00
C&NW: Stainless steel pocket knife, Zippo 15.00
CM&StP: Bronze locomotive clock, "Pioneer Limited," (rare) 1890s 500.00
CM&StP: Ornate letter opener, 5" long, "Chicago & Omaha Short Line" 25.00
CM&StP: Paperweight, electric locomotive 10250 on base, "To Puget Sound Electrified," silver finish (scarce) 135.00
CM&StP: Grizzly bear paperweight, "Gallatin Gateway to Yellowstone Park," bronze finish 85.00
COTTON BELT ROUTE: Medallion type paperwght, bronze, 3", logo, diesel, lightning bolt, flowers. Reverse side blank42.50
DM&N: Aluminum collapsible drinking cup, logo and Safety First on cover 15.00
ERIE: Trade card, 1890s. "Time And The Erie Wait For No Man" 12.50
FRISCO SYSTEM: Pocket mirror, train and advertisement on celluloid back 95.00*
GN: Safety razor in nickel-plated case, "Compliments of the New Oriental Ltd." 35.00

Pocket mirrors

IC: Jigsaw puzzle, Sioux City Iowa Corn Palace. Box dated 1889 (rare) 75.00
MKT: Cast-iron hinged matchbox, shape of old Katy logo150.00
MKT: Pocket diary, Indian Territory, Lady Katy on celluloid covers 37.50*

Pocket diary - front and backside

MP: Celluloid postage stamp case picturing Sunshine Special steam train, 1924 . . . . .20.00*

MP: Round cardboard fan, logo, advertising air-cooled name trains, 1930s 18.00

MP: Bottle opener, metal head, logo, steam engine on pearlized handle 15.00

MP: Pocket knife, Remington, logo, steam engine on pearlized handle 25.00

Northern Pacific Ry. baked potato inkwells

ROCK ISLAND: Glass paperweight, octagon, logo and advertisements, 1880s 85.00*

ROCK ISLAND: Soft plastic round case for coins, w/slit, imprinted logo 3.00

Celluloid postage stamp case

Glass paperweight

MONON ROUTE: Covered matchbox, alligator shape, bronze (rare) 400.00

NYC: Paperweight, streamlined locomotive 5445 on base, Britannia metal, silver finish, 1940s 150.00

NYC: Paperweight, locomotive 5200 on base, Britannia metal, silver finish, dated 1928 . . . . .200.00

NP: Teaspoon, silverplate, "Route Of The Great Big Baked Potato" 35.00

NP: Paperweight, upright bear on cube 4" tall, bronze. The Orme Co. 80.00

NP: Baked potato covered inkwell on base, pot metal, decorated (scarce) 350.00*

NP: Miniature bisque bible in original box, "Easter Greetings, 1912," Dining Car Dept 45.00

NP: Bronze letter opener, "Route Of The Great Big Baked Potato" 55.00

NP: Japanese folding fan, logo, ship and train, 1890s . .35.00

NP: Green felt pennant, "Route Of The Great Big Baked Potato," 75.00

PRR: Paperweight, cast iron, oval 3" x 5" PRR letters raised on topside, old 48.00

READING: Memo pad holder, steam locomotive on clip, copper finish, 1920s 55.00

SOO LINE: Tape measure, round celluloid case, logo & advertising, 1918 . . . . .22.00

SOO LINE: Tin serving tray, "Montana Success," 1906 . . . . .150.00

SOO LINE: Teaspoon, silverplate, Canadian Rockies in bowl, logo and advertising on handle .35.00

SOO LINE: Folding metal corkscrew, "Take The Soo For Fishing and Hunting" 25.00

SOO LINE: Desk paperweight, magnifying glass center, 1883-1958, Seventy-Fifth Anniversary 42.50

UP: Golf tees, 4 inside cardboard case imprinted w/logo and advertising copy 5.00

UP: Folding fan, "From Your Fans At Union Pacific Railroad" 5.00

WC: Ruler, 12", folding 3 piece, logo and advertising both sides, 1905 . . . . .30.00

ADVERTISING WALL POSTERS

The railroads used many colorful posters in the early years to advertise their trains and special travel features, which were posted in conspicuous places to catch the public's eye. Many of these did not survive the years. Value depends on condition, and a rarity will generally bring an exceptionally high price.

AT&SF: Entitled "Ten Little Navahos," children watching passenger train, recent........................5.00

B&M: Excursion trains to Forepaugh Wild West Shows, 2 sided, picturesque, 1890.........................125.00*

Railroad - circus poster

BCR&N: Bathing scene at Spirit Lake, Iowa's famous summer resort, Hotel Orleans in background, ca. 1885....150.00

BCR&N: Excursion poster promoting harvest excursions to the grain fields of the midwest, ca. 1900............50.00

CM: Indian on white horse with CM logo on shield, colorful (rare)
....450.00

GN: Photograph of Wm. Crooks and modern locomotive entitled "Yesterday & Today," 1862-1924, free exhibition at GN Station, Mpls................................35.00

NP: Entitled "Rodeo Parade" July 3-4-5, 1932, Montana-Wyoming, cowboys & Indians on horseback, 30 x 40"35.00*

NP: "The Dining Car Route To The Pacific Coast," Minn., N. Dak., Montana, Idaho, Oregon & Washington Territory, ca. 1887..130.00

NP: Scenery of Absoroka Mountains, Mont., passenger train in foreground by Gustav Krollman, ca. 1930s........25.00

Railroad - rodeo poster

PRR: Entitled "Washington, The City Beautiful," electric train foreground, capitol & buildings background, ca. 1930s35.00

SP: Passenger train illustration advertising that Klondikers should take the Shasta Route to Alaska, ca. 1898.......100.00

UP: "One Day Saved," The Overland Flyer, large Overland Route UP shield center, ca. 1890....................125.00

UP: Zion National Park, colorful scene, ca. 1950.....12.00

UP: Bryce Canyon National Park, Utah, colorful view, ca. 1950
....12.00

UP: WWII, entitled "In The Service Of Supply"......15.00

UP: WWII, entitled "Giving Them A Helping Hand"...15.00

WAB: Vase of roses, advertising the shortest line to St. Louis, Kansas City, the West and Southwest, ca. 1886...135.00

ART

Most nineteenth century original railroad art is owned by museums or is in private collections. Many artists from the early twentieth century produced railroad art that is now being offered for sale at various prices, depending on the fame of the artist. Original Currier & Ives railroad lithographs command very high prices. Other works, such as woodcuts, etchings, engravings, or reproductions of railroad subjects are priced according to their rarity. Old photographs of locomotives and railroad scenes are steadily increasing in value and are now finding their way into collections. Many of these various old pictures hung on the walls of depots and railroad offices. When found intact in their original frames, they usually bring a much higher price.

PAINTINGS AND DRAWINGS

Pen and ink drawing, 19½″ x 24½″, NP Ry's "North Coast
Limited," Helmut Kroening, 1901 . . . . 200.00
Watercolor, 11″ x 20½″, NYC & HR RR's "Empire State Express," Helmut Kroening, 1908 . . . . 350.00*

Original watercolor signed and dated 1908

Oil, 11½″ x 14½″ "Hezekiah Upjohn," railroad tycoon, A.
Sheldon Pennoyer, 1942 . . . . 400.00
Watercolor, 17¾″ x 24½″ "UP's Fast Mail, Sherman Hill, '55,"
Howard Fogg, 1960 . . . . 750.00

Watercolor, 12¾″ x 17½″, "Buffalo Hunt Excursion Train," Herb
Mott, 1961 . . . . 250.00
Pen and ink sketch, 6″ x 8″, "Old Time Atchison, Topeka &
Santa Fe Train," Herb Mott, 1961 . . . . 75.00
Pen and ink sketch, 7″ x 9″, engineer at the throttle in cab, Soo
Line advertisement, 1924 . . . . 95.00*

Pen and ink sketch - for newspaper ad

WOODCUTS, ETCHINGS AND ENGRAVINGS

Woodcut, 7″ x 14″, "The Village Depot," from *Harper's Week-
ly,* 1868, hand colored 50.00
Etching, 9¼″ x 15½″, NYNH & H RR Station, Springfield,
Conn., Geo. S. Payne, 1891 . . . . 200.00*
Engraving, 7¼″ x 10″, "Interior of An American Railway Car,"
from *Illustrated London News,* 1861 . . . . 20.00
Engraving, 7¼″ x 10¾″ "The Depot At Hexham,
Northumberland," England, 1836 . . . . 75.00

Original etching signed and dated 1891

BUILDER'S LITHOGRAPHS AND PHOTOGRAPHS

Litho, 22½″ x 28¼″, CCC RR's "Highland Light," Wm. Mason, Taunton, Mass., Ch. H. Crosby, Litho, Boston, ca. 1875, original frame. 1000.00*

Litho, 16¼″ x 26½″, 4-4-0 locomotive, The Hinckley Locomotive Works, Boston, C.H. Crosby & Co., Boston, ca. 1885, original frame. 500.00

Photo, plate 7″ x 16″, 4-4-0 locomotive, MStP & A, Manchester Locomotive Works, N.H. Kimball, Photographer, 1890, original frame. 135.00

Photo, plate 8″ x 15″, 4-8-2 locomotive, Pennsylvania 6800, Baldwin Locomotive Works, Phila. 1926, framed. . .50.00

Litho, 14″ x 19″, L.N. Rosenthal, funnel stack locomotive built by the M.W. Baldwin & Co., Phila., 1850s. 350.00

Builder's lithograph, ca. 1875

OLD PRINTS AND LITHOGRAPHS

Color print, 8″ x 11″, Northern Pacific Construction Train Stopped By Buffalos, 1875. *The St. Louis Globe Democrat*, April 27, 1902. . . . . .25.00

Reproduction, 22″ x 24″, Missouri Pacific's "Sunshine Special," Wm. Harnden Foster, ca. 1920s, original frame. . .175.00

Calendar print, 18″ x 23″, "Twentieth Century Limited-The Greatest Train In The World," Wm. Harnden Foster, 1922, framed. 75.00

Calendar print,16½″ x 23″, "The World's Greatest Highway, Horseshoe Curve," Grif Teller, 1934, framed. 65.00

Lithograph, 16″ x 24¾″, "View of Niagara Falls From Michigan Central Train," American Lithograhic Co., N.Y., 1903, original frame. 250.00

Lithograph, 18″ x 24″, "General, The Famous War Engine Of The Western & Atlantic RR," ca. 1920s, framed. . . .95.00

CURRIER & IVES LITHOGRAPHS

"American Express Train," Palmer del., lg. folio, 1864 . . . . .3500.00

"American Railroad Scene-Snowbound," sm. folio, 1871 . . . . .900.00

"The Express Train," J. Schutz del, small folio, N. Currier, 1853 . . . . .800.00

"The Lightning Express Train Leaving The Junction," Palmer del, large folio, 1863. . . . . .5500.00

"The Railroad Suspension Bridge-near Niagara Falls," small folio, N. Currier, 1856. . . . . .250.00

"Through To The Pacific," small folio, 1870. . . . . . . .500.00*

Currier & Ives lithograph, 1870

OLD PHOTOGRAPHS

Jackson colored photo, 1899

Brown monochrome, 16″ x 9¼″, "Engine Merrimac," Boston, Lowell & Nashua RR, Mason Machine Co., Taunton, Mass., 1868 . . . . 175.00

Photogravure etching, 20¾″ x 11½″, blue-black, "Empire State Express," Photogravure & Color Co., NY, 1906 . . . 125.00

Sepia, 8″ x 10″, CStPM&O's engine No. 157, with engineer and fireman posing, ca. 1900 . . . . 50.00

Color, 14″ x 21″, LS & MS's engine No. 604 pulling Twentieth Century Limited, Detroit Photographic Co., 1903 . . 150.00

Jackson photo, colored, 15″ x 21″, passenger train in Rio Las Animas Canyon, Colo., Detroit Photographic Co., 1899, original frame 135.00*

Colored, 8½″ x 15½″, Chicago & Northwestern's "400" on stone arch bridge, Minneapolis, ca. 1940s, original frame . 30.00

Colored, 11½″ x 12½″, Eastern Kentucky mountains along Louisville & Nashville Railroad's route, ca. 1920, original frame 45.00

Colored, 12½″ x 25½″, Frisco Line's "Firefly" streamlined steam passenger train, ca. 1930s, original frame 50.00

Colored, 14″ x 21″, Rock Island's "Rock Island Rocket," ca. 1945, original frame 35.00

Colored, 24″ x 36″, Wabash's streamlined "City of St. Louis," Forest Park, St. Louis, Mo., ca. 1950, original frame 45.00

BAGGAGE AND BRASS CHECKS

Various large rectangular brass checks are found that were used years ago to route travelers' baggage and railroad property pouches. These brass baggage checks came in matched sets on a leather strap. Today the pair is seldom found still intact on the original strap; the duplicate is usually missing, or only a single loose check is found. Many types of small brass tags, mostly round with a single hole in them, can also be found. These were used as time checks, parcel checks, tool checks, key tags, and so on. Many bear the maker's hallmark. Those from remote or obscure railroads are especially desirable and have the higher value.

A ST RR—"A.ST.R.R.#152," 1″ x 1 3/8″ oval key tag . . 8.00

B&O—"B.&O.R.R.", 1 3/8″ diameter, "O.R.D. 108" on reverse 12.00

B&O—"B.&O.R.R. LOCAL 39590," capitol dome logo, rect. 1½″ x 2¼″, "Am.Ry. Sup.Co. N.Y." 32.50

B&OSW—"B.&O.S.W.R.R., Cincinnati, O., Return To General Baggage Agent," rect. 2¾″ x 2⅛″, strap, "Am.Ry.S. Co. NY" 37.50

B&M—"BOSTON & MAINE RAILROAD, 58174 WAY," rect. 1⅜″ x 1¾″, "J. Robbins Mfg. Co. NY" 30.00

BCR&N—"Property of The Burlington Cedar Rapids & Northern Ry. Route, Cedar Rapids, Ia." 2⅛″ x 2½″, strap, "W.W. Wilcox Co., Chgo." 47.50

C&NW—"Property of THE NORTHWESTERN LINE" (logo) "C.St. P.M. & O. Ry." (below) "St. Paul, Minn., 2½″ x 2¼″, strap, "W. W. Wilcox Co., Chgo." 45.00

C&NW—"C.&N.W.RR. 633," time check, 1½″ x 1¾″, flat top, round bottom 15.00

CB&Q—Property of BURLINGTON ROUTE, Chicago," 2⅛″ x 2½″, "W.W. Wilcox Co., Chgo." 35.00

CM&PS—"C.M.&P.S. RY. Milwaukee, Wisc.," 2¼″ x 2½″, strap 42.50

CM&StP—"C.M.&St.P.RY. Milwaukee, Wisc." 2¼″ x 2½″, strap 30.00

CRI&P—"CHICAGO R I & PACIFIC RD. 6101," 2½″ x 1⅜″, "Thomas Pat. Feb. 9, 1867" 40.00*

GN—"G.N.Ry. 86," 1¼″ diameter, key tag . . 8.00

GB&W—"G.B.&W.R.R. and K.G.B.&W.R.R. 3527 Local," 1⅝″ x 2⅞″, "W.W. Wilcox Co., Chgo." 38.00

GT RY—"The Property of GRAND TRUNK RAILWAY SYSTEM" (logo) "Please return to this Co. as soon as possible." 2¼″ x 3″, strap 30.00

ERIE—"ERIE R.R. 416 J.C." 8 sided, 1″ across, "Am. Ry. Sup. Co. N.Y." 10.00*

FJ&G—"Gloversville and Northfield 5, via F J & G R R," 1½″ x 1¾″, J. Robbins, Boston 12.50

Checks on original straps · loose single

FJ&G— "Johnstown to Fonda 177 F.J.& G.R.R." pair on strap, one large, one smaller duplicate check, "J. Robbins, Boston" 38.00

H&StJ—"2377 H & St Jo RR," oval tag, 1½" x 1⅞" . .37.50

IC RR—"Return this check to ILL. CENT. R.R. Chicago," old diamond logo at bottom, 2⅛" x 2⅛", "W.W. Wilcox Co., Chgo." 36.00

MC—"The Property of The MICH.CEN.R.R.CO., Chicago, Ill. Please return to this Co., soon as possible." 1⅞" x 2¼", strap, "W.W. Wilcox Co., Chgo." 37.50

M&StL—"M. &St.L. Ry 307 local," 1½" x 1¾", strap.48.00

NYNH&H—"N.Y.N.H.&H.R.R. 20433 N H," 1⅝" diameter 15.00*

NYNH&H—"Saybrook Junc. and Narragansett Pier 1870, via NYNH&H, NYP&B, and NP RRs." pair on leather strap, one large, one smaller duplicate check, "J.J. Robbins, Boston" 75.00*

NP—"NORTHERN PACIFIC YELLOWSTONE PARK LINE" (logo) "local," 2¼" x 2½", strap, "Am. Ry. Sup. Co. N.Y." 45.00

OSL RR—"O.S.L.R.R. LOCAL, 01881," 1½" x 2", strap, "W.W. Wilcox, Chgo." 47.50*

P&R RY—Time check, "1503 P. & R.RY.CO" 1⅜" diameter, "Am.Ry.S.Co., N.Y." 12.50*

P&R RY—"PHIL. & READ.RY. from ChaddsFord Jct. Pa., Wilmington Br. local X23085," 1¼" x 2¼", "Am.Ry.S.Co., N.Y." 35.00

SP—"794 SOU.PAC.R.R. to C.S.&C.C.RY." 1½" x 2", strap, ...37.50

TC—"2449 TEXAS CENTRAL R.R. LOCAL," 1⅝" x 2", strap, "Poole Bros., Chgo." 35.00

UP—"Claim baggage at UN.PAC.RY. depot, Schuyler, Neb.25" pair on leather strap, one smaller duplicate check, "W.W. Wilcox, Chgo." 65.00

WAB—"WABASH R.R. CO. 4", heart shape tag, 1" x 1¼"12.00*

WC RY—"The property of the WISCONSIN CENTRAL RY., Milwaukee, Wisc. LOCAL," 1⅞" x 2¼", strap, "W.W. Wilcox, Chgo." 37.50

Miscellaneous brass checks

Baggage check enroute

Great Northern Railway children's china

Dining car napkins

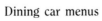

Dining car menus

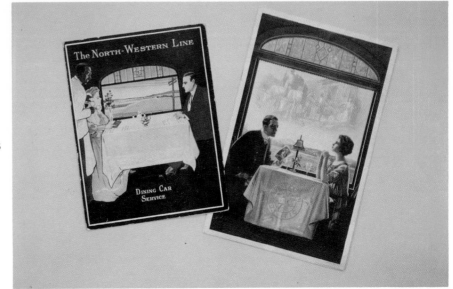

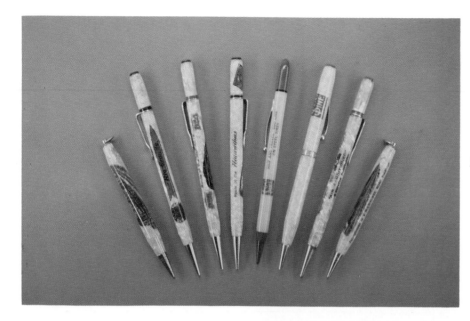

Mechanical pencils

Tape measure and folding ruler

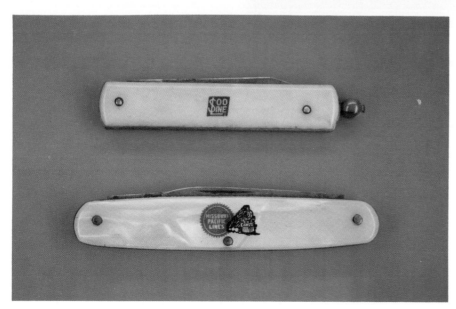

Pocket knives

Rare ink blotters

Timetable holder

Western Union depot items

Telegraph instruments - key, sounder and relay

Glass ashtrays

Brass and porcelain cuspidors

Cigarette lighters

Wallets and coin pouches

Coat lapel emblem pins

Lanterns with colored globes

Brass switchlocks and keys

Metalware - watering can, tallow pot and torch

Felt pennant

Railroad postcards

BOOKS

Many books have been written about the railroads since their beginning and up to the present time, covering their history, romance, classic trains, railroad tycoons, and so on. Some bring high prices. Many out-of-print books have increased in value due to their demand. Lucius Beebe's *Mr. Pullman's Elegant Palace Dining Car*, published in 1961, and sold at $17.50, now sells well over $50.00 a copy.

Railroad storybooks from yesteryear--such as the Big Little Books, Horatio Alger, Jr. and Allan Chapman Railroad Series books, and children's colorful railroad picture books—continue to interest the railroadiana collector, and their prices are steadily increasing. The books must be in fine condition, with all the pages intact, to bring a top price.

But most popular of all with collectors is *The Official Guide of the Railways,* in publication since 1867. Manuals, such as Poor's, Moody's, and others, are also in demand. Textbooks on the locomotive, cars and railway maintenance are sought after for their pictures and technical data. The earlier copies of these various books in fine condition bring high prices. Various rule books issued by the railroads down through the years are also collectible and priced according to their scarcity.

MANUALS

Bullinger's Postal And Shippers Guide, 1889 . . . . 75.00
Lyle's Official Railway Manual, 1869-1870 . . . . 130.00
Moody's Steam Railroads Manual, 1925 . . . . 45.00
Moody's Steam Railroads Manual, 1941 . . . . 30.00
Poor's Manual Of The Railroads Of The United States, 1874-1875
. . . . 125.00
Poor's Manual Of Railroads, 1888 . . . . 115.00
Poor's Manual Of Railroads, 1893 . . . . 100.00*
Poor's Manual Of Railroads, 1901 . . . . 85.00
Poor's Manual Of Railroads, 1906 . . . . 75.00*
Poor's Manual Of Railroads, 1912 . . . . 65.00*
Poor's Railroad And Bankers Manual, 1929 . . . . 50.00

Poor's Manuals

OFFICIAL GUIDES

The Official Guide Of The Railways, March, 1900 . . . . 100.00
The Official Guide Of The Railways, June, 1915 . . . . . . 75.00
The Official Guide Of The Railways, December, 1925 . . 65.00
The Official Guide Of The Railways, September, 1935 . 45.00
The Official Guide Of The Railways, October, 1945 . . . . 25.00

The Official Guide Of The Railways, October, 1955 . . . . 20.00
The Official Guide Of The Railways, October, 1962 . . . . 12.00
The Official Guide Of The Railways, June 1969, Golden Spike
Centennial Issue 10.00

RULE BOOKS

AT&SF—*Rules and Regulations,* 1959 . . . . 5.00
CGW—*Book Of Rules,* 1923 . . . . 15.00
C&NW—*Rules for the Government of the Operating Department,*
1929 . . . . 6.00
C&NW—*Instructions to Agents & Conductors,* 1881 . . . 15.00
CMStP&P—*Rules & Regulations for Conductors,* 1950 . . 5.00

IC—*Specifications Uniforming of Employees,* 1947 . . . . 10.00
GN—*Book of Rules,* 1908 . . . . 12.00
M&O—*Telegraph Code Book,* 1930 . . . . 15.00
NP—*Regulations, Operating Department,* 1899 . . . . 18.00
WC—*Rules, Regulations for Telegraphers,* 1903 . . . . . . 15.00

TEXTBOOKS

Car Builder's Dictionary—Third Thousand, 1881, 491 pages, 84
additional pages of advertisements in back 300.00

Catechism Of The Locomotive—M.N.Forney, 37th Thousand,
1890, 709 pages 35.00

EMD Operating Manual—G.N.RY Co., Passenger Locomotives, Apr. 15, 1945 . . . . .30.00

Hoxsie's Pocket Companion For Locomotive Engineers & Firemen—1875, 104 pgs 15.00

Locomotive Catechism—Robert Grimshaw, 13th Edition, 1894, 432 pages 20.00

Locomotive Cyclopedia—10th Edition, 1938, 1232 pages 125.00

Railway Engineering And Maintenance Cyclopedia—4th Edition, 1939, 1008 pages 110.00*

Roper's Hand-Book Of The Locomotive—1874, 324 pages 15.00

Science Of Railways—Marshall M. Kirkman, 1900 (vol. 1 of 12 volumes) 10.00

Text books

RAILROAD BOOKS

Commodore Vanderbilt—Wheaton J. Lane, 1942 . . . . . .12.50*

Development Of The Locomotive—Central Steel, 1925 . 15.00

History Of The Baldwin Locomotive Works—1831-1923 . . . . .45.00*

Railroad history books

History Of The Northern Pacific Railroad—Eugene V. Smalley, 1883 . . . . .85.00

Mr. Pullman's Elegant Palace Car—L. Beebe, 1961 . . . .75.00

Mixed Train Daily—Beebe & Clegg, 1953 (collector's edition, autographed) 40.00

Railroad Album—John O'Connell, 1954 . . . . .12.00

Railroading From The Head End—S. Kip Farrington, Jr., 1943 . . . . 15.00

Romance Of The Rails—Agnes C. Laut, 1929, vol. 1 and 2 . . . . .25.00*

Some Classic Trains—Arthur D. Dubin, 1975 . . . . .45.00

Story Of American Railroads—Stewart Holbrook, 1947 . 10.00

Story Of The B&O Railroad, 1827-1927—E. Hungerford, 1928, 2 volumes 65.00*

Stories Of The Railroad—John A. Hill, 1899 . . . . .15.00

The American Railway—Charles Scribner's Sons, N.Y., 1889, illustrated 150.00

The Rector Cook Book—Compliments of the Milwaukee Road, 5th Edition, 1928 . . . . .45.00

Wonders and Curiosities of the Railway—W.S. Kennedy, 1884 . . . . .20.00

WHITMAN BIG LITTLE BOOKS

Chuck Malloy, Railroad Detective—On the Streamliner, 1938 . . . . .15.00*

Union Pacific, 1939 . . . . .18.00*

BOY'S BOOKS

The Erie Train Boy—Horatio Alger, Jr 8.00*

Ralph And The Missing Mail Pouch—Allan Chapman (1 of 9 Railroad Series, 1924) 8.00*

My Railroad Book—Saml. Gabriel & Sons, 1914 . . . . . .27.50

On The Railroad—Saafield Co., 1936 . . . . .15.00

Railroad Book—McLoughlin Bros., 1909 . . . . .30.00

Railroad Picture Book—McLoughlin Bros., 1903 . . . . . .37.50

The Railway That Glue Built—Fred A. Stokes, 1908 . . .35.00

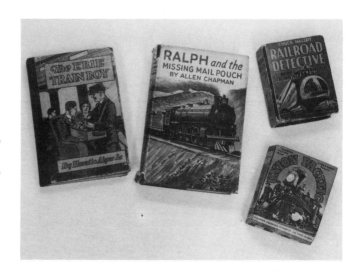

Boy's books

BREAST BADGES

Breast badges were worn by authorized railroad employees and other personnel connected with the railroads - police, watchmen, dining car stewards, baggage and railway mail service employees, and so on. The badge with the uncommon occupation embossed generally has a higher value. A word of caution: Reproduction breast badges are being made.

AT&SF—"810 SPECIAL OFFICER A.T.& S.F.RY.," six-pointed ball-tipped star, 2½", nickel plated, black letters, hmkd. F.W. Wilcox, Oak Park, Ill. 85.00

B&O—"BALTIMORE & OHIO R.R. RAILWAY POLICE," shield shape, nickel finish, raised letters, capitol dome embossed low center on pebbled field, not hmkd. 95.00*

Shield shape badge

C&A—"C & A RR SPECIAL POLICE," six-pointed star, 3½", nickel plated, black letters, hmkd. S.D. Childs & Co., Chicago 95.00

C&O—"C & O RY SPECIAL POLICE OFFICER," eagle top, 1½" x 2½", nickel finish, black letters, steam locomotive embossed on center disc., not hmkd. 85.00

D&H—"D & H CO. POLICE PATROLMAN," modified shield shape, w/side pillars, 2¼" x 2½", nickel finish, black letters, early locomotive raised inside circle, hmkd. C.G. Braxmar Co., Maiden Lane, N.Y. 125.00

GM&O—"ASST. SPECIAL AGENT, G.M. & O. RR CO.," six-pointed ball-tipped star, 2½", nickel plated, black letters, eagle atop shield emblem raised in center, hmkd. W.S. Darley & Co., Chicago 12 . . . . .105.00

GN—"GREAT NORTHERN RAILROAD," shield shape, 2¼" x 2¾", nickel plated, black letters, "SPECIAL OFFICER" on cut-out star center, hmkd. St. Paul Stamp Works. .135.00

GN—"G.N.RY. SPECIAL POLICE," six-pointed ball-tipped star, 2¾", nickel plated, black letters, hmkd. St. Paul Stamp Works 105.00

IC—"LIEUTENANT, CHIEF SPECIAL AGENT'S DEPT. I.C.R.R.," eagle atop sunburst, 1¾" x 2⅛", gold finish, black letters. "ILLINOIS CENTRAL R.RD.CO." around shield embossed in center. Pat. No.'s on back 105.00

IC—"POLICE 105 ILL. CENT. R.R.," six-pointed star, 3", nickel finish, black letters, not hmkd 85.00

KCT—"K.C. TERMINAL RY. CO.- KANSAS CITY, MO. 1915," circle, 2¼" dia., nickel finish, black letters, "SPECIAL 606 POLICE" on cut-out star center, hmkd. Allen Stamp & Seal Co., Kansas City 135.00

LS&MS—"L.S. &.M.S. RAILWAY D.C.S.," (dining car steward) shield shape, 1½" x 1¾", gold finish, black letters, hmkd.J.H. Fleharty, CLE.D.O 75.00

NYC&STL—"NICKEL PLATE PATROLMAN 121, N.Y.C. & ST.L.R.R.CO.," eagle atop shield, 1¾" x 2½", nickel finish, black letters, not hmkd 85.00

NP—"DEPUTY SHERIFF N. P. RY.," six-point star, 2½", nickel pltd, black letters, hmkd. St. Paul Stamp Works. . . .95.00

NP—"RAILROAD WATCHMAN, N.P.RY.," six-point star, 2½", nickel plated, black letters, hmkd. St. Paul Stamp Works 95.00

NP—"SPECIAL POLICE N.P. RY.," six-pointed star, 2½", nickel finish, black letters, not hmkd 85.00

NP—"RAILROAD WATCHMAN, N.P.RY.," six-pointed star, 2", nickel pltd, black letters, hmkd. St. Paul Stamp Works75.00

PRR—"P.R.R.CO. SERGEANT RAILWAY POLICE," shield shape, 2¼" x 3", nickel finish, engraved letters, State seal embossed in center, hmkd. S. G. Clover Co., successor to Am.Ry.S.Co., New York 130.00

Six-pointed star badge

POD—"POST OFFICE DEPARTMENT RAILWAY MAIL SER-
VICE 13415," embossed designs, oval center with "U.S."
monogram and stars, eagle at top, laurel leaves at bottom,
nickel finish, 2½" high, hmkd. Am.Ry.Supply Co., Park Place,
N.Y. 100.00
REA—"RAILWAY EXPRESS AGENCY POLICE," six-pointed
ball-tipped star with number in center, black indented letters,
nickel pltd, 2⅝", hmkd. Meyer & Wenthe, Chicago . 85.00
RI—"657 SERGEANT ROCK ISLAND LINES POLICE," six-
pointed ball-tipped star, 2½", nickel finish, black letters, not
hmkd 95.00

SAL—"CAPTAIN DETECTIVE POLICE," in blue enamel letters
on seven-pointed gold plated humped star, 2⅞",
"SEABOARD AIR LINE RAILROAD" in gold on black enamel
circle with red heart in center, not hmkd 150.00
StPUD—"ST. P.U.D. 438 BAGGAGE & MAILMAN," shield
shape, black indented letters, nickel plated, 2⅛" high, not
hmkd 47.50
WAB—"WABASH RY. CO. 729 POLICE," six-pointed tapered
star, 2¾", nickel plated, black letters, not hmkd . . . 95.00
WP—"THE WESTERN PACIFIC R.R.CO. CALIFORNIA,
RAILROAD AND STEAMBOAT POLICE 71," six-pointed
star, 3¼", nickel plated, black letters, not hmkd . . 150.00*

BROTHERHOOD ITEMS

Brotherhood items are a segregated specialty that includes badges, celluloid pin-back buttons, coat lapel buttons and pins, and other
miscellaneous items. Of particular interest are the colorful reversible lodge badges with satin ribbons attached. These were worn at
conventions, funerals and in parades. The coat lapel buttons issued to members of the Brotherhood for years of service are also noteworthy;
some of these were made of solid gold. Note: Brotherhood magazines are included in the magazine section.

Lodge badges - fronts

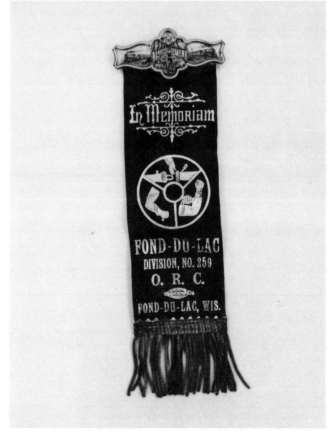

Lodge badge - backside

BADGES, LODGE—red-white-green gold fringed satin ribbon (backside black) attached emblem ornaments.

"B. OF L.F. & E.—Taylor Lodge No. 175, Newark, Ohio," 9" x 2¾" 30.00
"B. OF R.R. TRAINMEN—Killington Lodge No. 297, Rutland, Vt." 8½" x 2¾" 30.00*

"O.R.C.—Div. 259, Fond du Lac, Wisc.," 9½" x 2¾" . 25.00*
"VETERANS ASSOCIATION, GREAT NORTHERN RY. Memoriam to James J. Hill, Feb. 23, 1913," purple gold fringed satin ribbon, 9" x 2¾" 20.00

BADGES, CONVENTION—The pinclasp bar has the member's name, with or w/o red-white-green satin ribbon attached. The hanging medallion has raised letters and designs, along with trains, buildings, etc.

Convention badges

A.R.S.B. & B.—Pinclasp has enamelled emblem, ornate silver medallion has a train depot and bridge in relief, also "Railway Superintendents of Bridges & Buildings," hmkd. C.G. Braxmar Co., Maiden Lane, N.Y 15.00*
B.L.E.—Pinclasp has name, rectangular silver medallion has front end of passenger train in relief, also "Sixth Triennal Convention, Cleveland, June, 1930," hmkd. Bastian Bros., Rochester, N.J. 20.00
B. OF R.T.—Pinclasp has depot, state seal and "Columbus, May 1909," embossed. Round silver medallion has passenger train, flags in relief, and "9th Biennial Convention Brotherhood of Railroad Trainmen." Satin multi-color ribbon, hmkd. Whitehead & Hoag, Newark, N.J. 32.50*
O.R.C.—Pinclasp has name, attached multi-color ribbon; silver medallion has enameled Order of Railway Conductor's emblem, pass. train on stone arch bridge, with words "38th Session Grand Division, Minneapolis, May 1925" in relief, hmkd. Greenduck Co., Chgo. 30.00*
B. OF R.T.A.—Pinclasp has name, attached multi-color ribbon. Gold medallion has 3 enameled shields at top, pass. train raised in center circle w/words "Am.Ass'n. of General Passenger and Ticket Agents, St. Paul, Sept. 1911," hmkd. Chas. M. Robbins, Attelboro, Mass. 25.00

LAPEL BUTTONS AND PINS

"B. OF R.R. BRAKEMEN"—gold brakewheel and letters on black enamel 10.00*
"B.R.C.A." (Brotherhood Railway Carmen of America)—hammer and wrench crossed in center, gold on black 14.00
"B. OF R.R. CLERKS"—green and red pen and pencil on white background 8.00
"B. OF R.C." (Brotherhood of Railway Clerks)—25 year service pin, red pencil and green quill on white, 10-K 22.50
"B. OF L.E. HONORARY C.I.D."—2 steam engines in center, 10-K 30.00
"B.L.F. & E."—20 years continuous membership, enameled red-green-white logo triangle, round pin, 10-K 20.00
"B. OF L.F. & E."—cut-out steam engine, black on gold 25.00*

Pinbacks and coat lapel emblem pins

"B. OF R.R.F.H. and B.OF R.C." (Brotherhood of Railway Freight Hdlrs & Rwy Clerks)—dolly & hook, pen & ledger...8.00*

"B. OF R.R. TICKET AGENTS"—ticket validator, blue enameled, fancy edge........................30.00

"B OF R.T.—BROTHERHOOD RAILROAD TRAINMEN," in red around white, brakewheel with big green T, 15 years, gold wreath around............................15.00

PINBACK BUTTONS

"B. OF A.R.E.E."—May 1919, Local 21, baggage car, blue, 1" diameter.................................15.00

"O.R.C."—Order of Railway Conductors, caboose, 1⅛" diameter 6.00

"B. OF L.E.OF N.Y.C.S."—Empire State Express, Mch. 20, 1900, 1¾" dia...................................45.00*

"B. OF L.F. & E."—member, organized 1873, triangle emblem, ⅞" diameter.................................5.00

"B. OF R.R. TRAINMEN"—tri-colored BRT monogram, 1" diameter.................................4.00

"B. OF R.R. TRAINMEN"—25th Anniversary, 1883-1908, BT RR emblem, 1¾".........................15.00*

PAPER AND MISCELLANEOUS

B.L.E.—Cigarette lighter, plastic bottom, metal top. Scripto 10.00

B. OF L.F.—Invitation to annual ball, 1888, locomotive on cover 12.50

B. OF R.R. TRAINMEN—Invitation to annual ball, 1912, trainman on cover............................10.00

EMBOSSING SEAL—Bro. of Locomotive Engineers, 1889 ....75.00

BUTTONS AND EMBLEM PINS

Uniform buttons have always been popular with the railroadiana collector. These had the name or initials of the railroad embossed on them, and came in a gold or silver finish with a flat or domed front. They also were made with the occupation designated on them, such as "Conductor," "Brakeman," "Porter," etc. Most were in the standard coat and sleeve sizes, but other sizes can also be found. Most had a loop back, but they were also made with a patented lock-on back, snapping over the existing sewn-on button, or in the case of the cap button, a pronged back to push through the fabric. Prices shown are for authentic old buttons in very fine condition, with the manufacturer's or supplier's name stamped on the backside. Restrikes are being made today, so careful study of all buttons is required.

Railroad employees wore various coat lapel emblem pins issued them for years of service, and also wore official insignias on their uniforms. Many of these had enamel inlay work, finely detailed in design, and were either gold finish or real gold. Some collectors specialize in these colorful coat lapel emblem pins.

Railroadmen's work clothing often had brass buttons sewn on them with stamped designs connected with their occupation, as a locomotive, lantern, semaphore, or a railroad-related name. Some of these buttons date back before the turn of the century, and few are later than 1930. These work clothing buttons are harder to find than the uniform buttons and bring higher prices.

KEY TO ABBREVIATIONS

LGD—Large gold dome
SGD—Small gold dome

LGF—Large gold flat
SGF—Small gold flat

P—Pronged back for cap
FOX—Patent snap-over back

LSD—Large silver dome
SSD—Small silver dome

LSF—Large silver flat
SSF—Small silver flat

Note: All buttons listed show the actual marking (railroad initials or name) on the frontside and the name of the manufacturer or supplier stamped on the backside.

UNIFORM BUTTONS

"A C & S RR, SHORE FAST LINE"—SSF, Wanamaker & Brown, Phil 3.50
"A C L"—SSF, Superior Quality 2.00
"ATLANTIC & GREAT WESTERN RR"—LGF, D. Evans & Co. Attelboro, Mass. (rare) 35.00
"B C E R"—LGF, J.R. Gaunt & Sons, Ltd., Montreal . . .6.00
"BIG FOUR"—LSF, Scovill Mfg. Co., Waterbury 4.50
"BOSTON ELEVATED RAILWAY"—LGF, Boston Elevated Railway 5.00
"BOSTON & MAINE RR"—SSD, maltese cross center, Scovill Mfg. Co., Waterbury 4.50
"CHESAPEAKE & OHIO RAILWAY CO"—w/C&O monogram center, LSD, Henderson & Co., Phila., Pa 8.50
"C G W" in script—LGF, Scovill Mfg. Co., Waterbury . .7.50
"C M & St.P RY"—LGF, Chas. Rubens & Co., Chgo . . .6.00
"C M & St.P"—LGF, Browning King & Co 5.00
"C M & St.P"—SGF, The Royal Tailors, Chgo., U.S.A . .4.00
"C M & St.P"—SSF, Cumner Jones & Co., Boston 4.00
"C M & St.P & P"—SSF, P, no maker's name 5.00*

Uniform buttons · Fox Patent, cap and toggle pin types

"C St.P M & O"—LSF, Chicago Uniform & Cap Co 8.00
"C St.P M & O"—SGD, P, no maker's name 6.00
"C St.P M & O"—SSF, Superior Quality 6.00
"D. P. ELECTRIC LINES"—(Dan Patch) LGF, The Palace, Mpls. (scarce) 25.00
"D & H"—LSD, American Button Co., Newark, N.J 4.00
"D & R G W"—LSD, Superior Quality, made in England4.00
"E & T H"—LSF, E. F. Schreimer Bros. & Co., Cincinnati, O 8.00
"ERIE"—LGD, Scovill Mfg. Co., Waterbury 6.00
"ERIE"—LSD, Scovill Mfg. Co., Waterbury 5.00
"GRAND TRUNK R.R."—w/GT monogram center, LGF, Ernest J. Scott, Montreal 10.00
"GRAND RAPIDS RAILWAY CO."—in script, SGF, Waterbury Button Co 4.00
"GREAT NORTHERN RY. LINE"—w/GN monogram center, LGF, Waterbury Button Co., Waterbury, Conn 8.00
"G S & F"—SSF, Waterbury Button Co 4.00
"G T R-CONDUCTOR,"—w/beaver animal in oval, LGD, Waterbury Button Co., Waterbury, Conn 22.50*

"HOUSTON & TEXAS CENTRAL RAILWAY"—w/H&TC monogram center, LSD, Waterbury Button Co., Waterbury, Conn. 12.00
"H. & B. T. R.R."—SGD, Wannamaker & Brown, Phil .6.00
"I C"—LSF, Superior Quality 3.00
"I.C.St.Ry Co"—LSD, D. Evans & Co., Attleboro, Mass .8.00
"INDIANAPOLIS STREET RAILWAY CO."—LGF, C.A. Bropny, Aurora, Ill 6.00
"I R T CO"—LGD, Superior Quality 6.00
"Lackawanna R.R."—w/monogram center, LSD, Scovill Mfg. Co. 12.00
"L S & M S"—SSD, Scovill Mfg. Co 5.00
"M & St L"— LGF, Cumner Jones & Co., Boston 8.00
"M & St L"—LSD, Fox, no maker's name 7.00
"M & St L"— SSD, Fox, no maker's name 5.00
"MISSOURI KANSAS & TEXAS"—LGD, Steele & Johnson, Waterbury 15.00

Dual marked · railroad and occupation

"MISSOURI PACIFIC LINES"—w/buzz-saw edge, LGF, Superior Quality 3.00
"N.Y.C."—LGF, Scovill Mfg. Co., Waterbury, Conn 3.00
"N.Y.C. & H R R R"—LGD, Scovill Mfg. Co., Waterbury 7.00
"N.Y.C. & St.L.R.R.Co."—w/Nickel Plate in center, LSD, Extra Quality 15.00
"N.Y. LAKE ERIE & W.R.R.CO."—w/BRAKEMAN center, LGD, Scovill Mfg. Co., Waterbury 22.50*
"N P"—(monogram), LSF, Fox, Scovill Mfg. Co 4.00
"NORTHERN PACIFIC"—w/NP center, SGD, Scovill Mfg. Co6.00
"NORTHERN INDIANA RAILWAY CO"—in script, LGF, Superior Quality 9.00
"O W"—(logo), LGF, Scovill Mfg. Co., Waterbury, Conn 4.00

Occupational titles

"O & W"—center, New York Ontario & Western Railway around edge, Jacob Reed's Sons, Phil 12.00

"P & L E"—LGD, Horstmann, Philadelphia 6.00

"P M"—LGD, Marshall Fields & Co 6.00

"P R R"—in Keystone logo, LSD, American Ry. Supply Co., N.Y. 5.00

"P R R"—LSD, American Ry. Supply Co., 24 Park Place, N.Y. 7.00

"PENNSYLVANIA CO."—w/monogram center, LSD, Waterbury Button Co 8.00

"PORTLAND RAILROAD"—LGF, Scovill Mfg. Co., Waterbury 5.00

"READING LINES"—w/R Co. in diamond, center, LGD, Superior Quality 5.00

"R & I RY."—LSF, Waterbury Button Co., Conn 8.00

"ROCK ISLAND LINES"—w/star center, LGF, Pettibone Bros. Cinn., O 4.00

"St J Ry"—in rectangle, LGF, F E Chheimer Bros. Co., Cincinnati, O 8.00

"St L & O R"—w/CONDUCTOR around edge, car in oval below, LGD, Waterbury Button Co., Waterbury, Conn 22.00*

"St P & S. C. R. R."-w/CONDUCTOR, star center, LGD, Extra Quality 25.00

"SALT LAKE"—LSD, B. Pasquale Co., S. Fran., Cal . .15.00

"S P"—entwined letters, LGD, Superior Quality 3.00

"SOUTHERN"—around center circle, LGD, Jacob Reed's Sons, Phila 4.00

"SOO LINE"—LSD, Fox, no maker's name 5.00*

"SOO LINE"—SGD, Fox, no maker's name 4.00

"S U RyS"—LGD, Superior Quality 6.00

"TOPEKA RAILWAY CO."—w/TR monogram center, LGF, Waterbury Button Co., Waterbury, Conn 6.00

"TORONTO RAILWAY COMPANY"—w/beaver animal center, LGD, J.S. Russell, Toronto 8.00

"TORONTO & YORK RADIAL RY."—w/TYR letters center, LGD, J.R. Gaunt & Sons Ltd., Montreal 10.00

"UNION PACIFIC"—LGD, American Ry. Supply Co. N.Y.4.00

"UNION PACIFIC"—LSD, F. G. Clover Co., New York .4.00

"U T C of IND"—LGF, Supreme Quality 6.00

"VANDALIA LINES"—w/VL monogram center, LGD, Waterbury Button Co 18.00

"WABASH"—LSD, Fox, no maker's name 8.00

"W C RY"—LGD, Fox, no maker's name 12.00

"WEST CHICAGO St. R.R. CO."—w/WC monogram center, LGD, Waterbury Button Co 10.00

MISCELLANEOUS AND EXPRESS

"AGENT"—LGD, Scovill Mfg. Co., Waterbury 5.00*

"AGENT"—LSD, Horstmann Bros. & Co., Philada 6.00

"BAGGAGE MAST"—spokewheel center, LSD, Waterbury Button Co 8.00*

"BRAKEMAN"—star center, LGD, Scovill Mfg. Co., Waterbury 6.00

"BRAKEMAN"—LSF, Fechheimer Bros. Co., Cincinnati, Ohio 5.00*

"CONDUCTOR"—LGF, Chas. Rubens & Co., Chicago . .5.00

"CONDUCTOR"—LSD, Charles Rubens & Co., Chicago 5.00*

"CONDUCTOR"—star center, LGD, Pettibone Mfg. Co., Cincinnati 6.00

"INSPECTOR"—SGF, Superior Quality, made in Eng . . .5.00

"MOTORMAN"—spokewheel center, LGD, Cumner Jones & Co., Boston 5.00

"PORTER"—star center, LSD, Waterbury Button Co., Conn 4.00

"PULLMAN"—LSF, Superior Quality 3.00

"PULLMAN"—SSF, P, Superior Quality 2.00

"P.P.C.Co."—within wreath, LSD, Henry V. Allien & Co., N.Y. 18.00

"ADAMS EXPRESS COMPANY"—in rectangle, LGF, Scovill Mfg. Co., Waterbury 10.00

"AMERICAN EXPRESS CO."—shield in center, LGD, Waterbury Button Co 12.00*

Express and Palace car

"NATIONAL EXPRESS CO."—"N" in center circle, LGD, Scovill
  Mgf. Co., Waterbury....................10.00
"NEW YORK & BOSTON LINES EXPRESS"—LSD, Scovill Mfg.
  Co., Waterbury......................15.00

"RAILWAY MAIL SERVICE"—"P O D" center, LGD, Scovill
  ....9.00
"WAGNER PALACE CAR CO"—winged wheel center, LGD,
  Henry V. Allien & Co., New York..............20.00*

COAT LAPEL EMBLEM PINS

ATLANTIC COAST LINE—"Safety Committeeman," white on
  green....................................20.00
B & O—Veteran, white capitol dome in blue "V" on gold25.00
BURLINGTON ROUTE—"Safety First" around logo in center
  ....25.00
C.M. & St. P RY.—"Veteran, 25 years," blue on gold..35.00
CHICAGO MILWAUKEE ST. PAUL & PACIFIC—around
  Milwaukee Road logo.....................10.00*

Coat lapel emblem pins

C. & N.W. RY. CO.—"Veterans Association" around logo
  ....18.00

COTTON BELT ROUTE—logo, silver and blue.......35.00*
DULUTH & IRON RANGE RR CO.—"Get The Safety Spirit,"
  Indian profile (scarce).....................75.00
GREAT NORTHERN—goat logo, pre-1935..........30.00*
ILLINOIS CENTRAL RAILROAD—around "Safety Always First"
  ....25.00
LAKE SHORE & MICHIGAN SOUTHERN RY.—mail sack
  emblem, 10-K.............................37.50
MINNEAPOLIS & ST. LOUIS RY. CO.—"The Peoria Gateway"
  ....45.00*
MISSOURI PACIFIC—red buzz-saw logo, "Booster Club"20.00
NEW YORK CENTRAL LINES—gold on black, oval..18.00
NORFOLK & WESTERN RY.—"Veteran," steam locomotive,
  10-K....................................30.00
NORTHERN PACIFIC—monad logo, 10-K..........25.00
NORTHERN PACIFIC—monad logo, 10-K "45 years" diamond
  gemstone 75.00
NORTHERN PACIFIC—monad logo, 10-K, "35 years" ruby
  gemstone 50.00
OMAHA RAILWAY—"Safety veteran - 25 years no injury"30.00
PENNSYLVANIA RAILROAD—"Veteran," Keystone logo
  ....22.50
UNION PACIFIC—shield logo, "The Overland Route".27.50*
Y. & M.V. RAILROAD—around "Safety Always First" (scarce)
  ....35.00

OFFICIAL LAPEL INSIGNIAS (matched pairs)

"BURLINGTON ROUTE"—rectangular logo.......30.00-set
"C M & St.P"—gold cut-out letters..............38.00-set*
"C & N W"—gold cut-out letters................15.00-set*
"KANSAS CITY SOUTHERN LINES"—logo, gold on red
  ....28.00-set
"THE MILWAUKEE ROAD"—logo, red canted box logo
  ....20.00-set
"THE NORTHWESTERN LINE, F.E. & M.V.R.R."—blue and
  black logo (rare).........................50.00-set
"OMAHA" gold cut-out letters..................38.00-set
"ROCK ISLAND"—logo, gold letters on black.....25.00-set*

Lapel insignias

COAT SLEEVE SERVICE BARS AND STARS

These ornaments were worn by uniformed passenger conductors,
brakemen, flagmen, porters, station masters, gatemen and others.
Each bar on the sleeve represents 5 years of service. After 5 bars,
a star would be placed just above the row of bars to represent
5 additional years of service.

G.N.RY.—¼″ x ⅞″ gold bar......................20.00
G.N.RY.—¼″ x ⅞″ silver bar....................18.00
ROCK ISLAND—¼″ x ¾″ gold bar...............18.00
ROCK ISLAND—¼″ x ¾″ silver bar.............16.00
SANTA FE—5⁄16″ x ⅞″ gold bar...................15.00
SANTA FE—5⁄16″ x ⅞″ silver bar.................12.00
UNMARKED—¼″ x ⅞″ gold bar.................4.00
UNMARKED—¼″ x ⅞″ silver bar...............4.00
UNMARKED—¾″ gold star......................5.00
UNMARKED—¾″ silver star.....................5.00

Coat sleeve ornaments

RAILROADMEN'S WORK CLOTHES BUTTONS

"CONES BOSS"—embossed lantern, brass...........6.00*
"FAST LIMITED"—embossed letters, brass..........5.00*
"MAIN LINE SPECIAL"—embossed locomotive, brass..9.00
"OSHKOSH BRAND"—embossed locomotive, brass....7.00
"PAYMASTER"—embossed pay car, brass...........12.00
"RAILROAD KING"—embossed letters, brass........5.00*
"RAILROAD MAN"—embossed profile, brass.........8.00
"RAILROAD SIGNAL"—embossed semaphore, brass...6.00
"ROUNDHOUSE"—embossed roundhouse, brass......12.00
"SWOFFORD'S MOGUL"—embossed locomotive, brass.6.00
"TEN WHEELER"—embossed locomotive, brass.......8.00
"THE ENGINEER"—embossed locomotive, brass......9.00*
"THE RAILROAD"—embossed locomotive, brass......8.00
"UNTITLED"—embossed locomotive, brass...........3.50*

Work clothing buttons

CALENDARS

The railroads gave away many thousands of calendars down through the years, which are now being collected. The rarities are the early color-lithographed calendars from the last quarter of the nineteenth century, which bring very high prices. Of special interest to the collector today are the New York Central and Pennsylvania Railroad calendars illustrating their famous "Name trains" of the steam era. Closely following these are Great Northern's Indian series, done by Winold Reiss in the 1920s and 1930s. There are a great many others with interesting railroad subjects, all very collectible and selling well. Those that have been kept in their original mint condition have the highest value.

AT&SF—1954, Navajo shepherdess, 13¼″ x 24¼″, all monthly pages intact................................12.50
B&O—1827-1927, Centennial 20¾″ x 28½″, painting depicts laying the first stone, all monthly pages intact......37.00
B&O—1948, large single sheet 21″ x 31½″, picture has capitol dome, map, steam and diesel trains, 12 months printed on bottom half................................22.50

BN—1971, large single sheet 26″ x 42″, photo of diesel train along Columbia River, 12 mo. printed on bottom half 8.00
C&A—Four tri-monthly cardstock pages issued for the Louisiana Purchase Expo. St. Louis, Mo., 1904. Each page depicts a girl w/sword in various fencing positions........100.00*

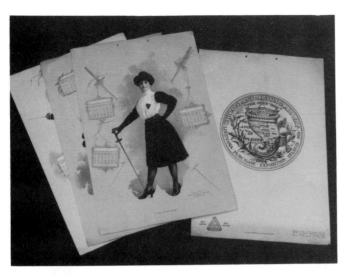

Early four-page cardstock calendar complete

G.N.Ry. Indian series monthly calendars

C&O—1948, "Here Comes Your Train, Chessie," 14″ x 24″, all monthly pages intact 16.00

C&NW—July 1900, June 1901, 8½″ x 10½″, scenes of picturesque Milwaukee on each page, all monthly pages intact 50.00

C & NW—1937, large Northwestern Line logo, 15″ x 23″, all monthly pages intact 20.00

C&NW—1941, streamliner 400 on stone arch bridge, 18″ x 24″, all monthly pages intact 15.00

CB&Q—1939, single sheet 18″ x 27″ pictures steam and diesel trains against a mountain background w/vignette of covered wagons in the sky, mint 30.00

CGW—Quarterly cardstock page from 1900 calendar for months of April, May, June, picturing an Apache Indian girl .35.00

CK&N—"Rock Island Route" 1889, cardstock sheet, 14″ x 22″, picture of girl and passenger train. Several monthly pages gone (rare) 135.00

CRI&P—1888, cardstock sheet 14″ x 22″, picture of "A. Man" with umbrella and valise, all monthly pages intact . .125.00

D&RGW—1944, train in Royal Gorge, Colo., 15″ x 25¾″, all monthly pages intact 15.00

FEC—1944, map of Florida and freight train, 14″ x 24″, all monthly pages intact 10.00

FRISCO—1962, large single cardstock sheet 22″ x 28″, top depicts map of system and diesel freight train, 12 months printed below 8.50

GN—May, 1928, one month cardstock sheet, 10¼″ x 22″, portrait of Chief Two Guns White Calf by Winold Reiss 35.00

GN—June, 1929, one month cardstock sheet, 10¾″ x 20½″, painting of Many Glacier Hotel, Lake McDermott by Adolph Heinze 30.00

GN—February, 1930, one month cardstock sheet, 10″ x 22″, portrait of Long Time Pipe Woman by Winold Reiss . . .25.00

GN—1931, complete set 12 months, Indian portraits by Winold Reiss 200.00*

IC—1951, One Hundred Years Of Progress, 1851-1951, medallion, 18″ x 27¼″, mint 25.00

M&StL—1945, single sheet 18″ x 24½″, color photo of steam locomotive No. 627 pulling freight train, all monthly pages intact 45.00

MP—Perpetual tin wall calendar, 12½″ x 19″, color picture of new diesel streamliner, "Eagle," all date cards intact 125.00

MP—Perpetual tin wall calendar, 12½″ x 19″, color litho of steam train 'Sunshine Limited," all date cards intact 150.00*

Perpetual tin wall calendar

NYC—1924, single sheet, 25″ x 26½″, painting "As The Centuries Pass In The Night" by Wm. Harnden Foster, mint, fly leaf attached..............................100.00*

NYC 1924 calendar, mint, fly leaf intact

NYC—1923, single sheet 25″ x 26½″, painting "The Greatest Train In The World," The 20th Century Ltd. by Wm. Harnden Foster, mint...........................75.00

NYC—1926, single sheet, 25″ x 26½″, painting, "A National Institution," The 20th Century Ltd. by Walter L. Greene, mint
....75.00

NP—1970, single sheet 20½″ x 25¾″, scene of diesel freight train emerging from tunnel, 12 months printed below.... 6.00

PRR—1924, cardstock desk calendar, 3½″ x 4½″, "Broadway Limited," shows front end of engine in Keystone logo, monthly pages intact..........................15.00

P RR—1935, single sheet 29″ x 28½″, painting "The World's Greatest Highway-Horseshoe Curve" by Grif Teller, all monthly pages intact...........................65.00

P RR—1947, single sheet, 29″ x 28½″, painting "Working Partners" by Grif Teller, all monthly pages intact......50.00

P RR—1953, single sheet, 29″ x 28½″, painting "Crossroads Of Commerce," by Grif Teller, all monthly pages intact.45.00

SANTA FE—1929, cardstock panel, 13¾″ x 13″, "The Blanket" by E.I. Couse, N.A., all monthly pages gone.......22.50

UP—1869-1969, Centennial, 19″ x 24″, wall type, 8 pages with 16 railroad paintings by Howard Fogg............15.00

CANS, TORCHES & METALWARE

Of the large variety of cans used on the railroads, the most popular with the collector is the engineer's classic long-spout oiler. Next are the various types of kerosene cans. Those from the steam era, marked with the name of the railroad, are much in demand. Those unmarked, or with only the manufacturer's name on them, have less value. Cans badly dented or rusted must be discounted.

Oil burning torches were used in the old days to provide a light while working around the locomotive and in the roundhouse. They were made with a wick, in a variety of styles, shapes and sizes. A great many were not railroad marked; some were marked with only the name of the manufacturer. Those railroad marked and in fine condition are worth more.

ENGINEER'S LONG SPOUT OILERS

B&O RR—Embossed on front, 30″ tall, stop flow lever, "J-Urbana"..................................30.00

CRI&P RY—Stamped on bottom, 31½″ tall, stop flow lever, "Anthes Force"..............................45.00*

DL&W RY—Embossed on side, 29½″ tall, stop flow lever, "J-Urbana".................................42.50

GN RY—Incised on handle, 30½″ tall, stop flow lever, "Eagle"
....47.50

NP RY—Embossed on bottom, 30½″ tall, stop flow lever, "J-Urbana".................................37.50*

PRR—Embossed Keystone logo front, 26″ tall, no lever, cap only, "J-Urbana"..............................27.50*

SOO RR—Embossed on bottom, 28½″ tall, stop- flow lever, "Handlan"..................................38.00*

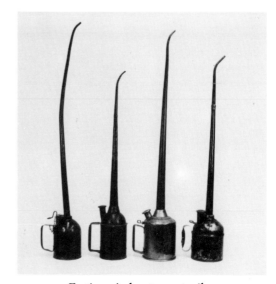

Engineer's long spout oilers

SHORT SPOUT OILER

GNR—Embossed on side tag, 9″ spout, pat. Nov. 12, 1912, "Eagle".....................................35.00

NYC—Stamped around top, 4″ spout, "Eagle".......18.00

KEROSENE OR SIGNAL OIL CANS

AT&SF RY—Embossed near base, ribbed sides, 10½″ high, 7″ diameter bottom.............................27.50

CB&Q RR CO. ICC 2A—Stamped on top, ribbed sides, iron spout, 12″ high, 9″ diameter bottom, "J-Urbana".......30.00

CStPM&O—Embossed tag rear, 9″ high, 6½″ diameter base, "Eagle".....................................37.50

GN RY—Stamped side of dome, 8½″ high, 5¼″ diameter bottom, hand grip, bail, "J-Urbana".................27.50*

GN RY—Embossed side of dome, 13″ high, 8″ diameter bottom, hand grip, wood spool bail....................30.00

NPR—Embossed at side, inverted funnel type, 6″ high, 7″ diameter, "J-Urbana"..........................25.00

Kerosene cans

WATER CANS, GALVANIZED

BURLINGTON ROUTE—Embossed logo on front, 9¼″ high, 7½″ diameter bottom........................35.00

CMStP&P RR—Embossed at side, 9¼″ high, 7¼″ diameter bottom.....................................20.00

DSS&A RR—Embossed side of dome, 12″ high, 8″ diameter, lid only...................................45.00*

NYCS—Embossed on side, tea kettle shape, 7″ high, 8¼″ x 10⅞″, oval bottom..........................30.00

NP RY—Embossed on side, 14″ high, 8½″ diameter bottom, wood spool bail, hinged lid....................25.00

SOO LINE—Embossed side of dome, 12″ high, 8″ diameter bottom, lid only..............................35.00

Water can

TORCHES

Torches

B&O RR—Embossed on handle, teapot style, 4½″ high, 5″ handle, "Peter Grey, Boston".....................25.00
BURLINGTON ROUTE—Embossed side logo, teapot style, 4¾″ high, 9″ handle.............................45.00
C&NW RY—Bottom marked, cone-shaped torch with hook, wick, 9½″ tall, "J-Urbana".......................30.00
CGW RY—Embossed bottom, coffeepot style, 7″ high, 12″ long, bail hook.................................42.50
CM&StP—Bottom stamped, long spout, teapot type, grip handle, 6″ tall..................................35.00*
GN RY—Bottom mkd, candle type, height 13″, all brass 65.00*
M&StL RR—Side embossed, conical type, height 14″..38.00
MO.PAC.RR—Embossed on side plate, long handle torch, wick, "Eagle".......................................45.00
SOO LINE—Embossed side logo, teapot style, 4¾″ high, 9″ handle....................................50.00*
UP RR—Side marked, cast iron torch, wick, 10″ tall, "Dayton Malleable"...................................37.50
UNION PACIFIC—Embossed on side plate, long handled torch, wick, "Eagle"...............................40.00

TALLOW POTS

C&NW RY—Embossed on bottom, teapot style, 7″ high, 5″ x 7¼″ oval base, "J-Urbana".....................25.00*
CB&Q RR—Embossed on bottom, teapot style, 7¼″ high, 5″ x 8″ oval base, "Gem".......................35.00
GNR—Embossed on side tag, teapot style, 6″ high, 5¼″ x 7½″ oval base.................................30.00*
M&StLRR—Embossed on side, coffeepot style, side handle, 7½″ high, 5″ x 8½″ oval base.....................37.50
ROCK ISLAND LINES—Embossed on side, coffeepot style, 7″ high, 5″ diameter base.......................22.50
SOO LINE—Embossed on both sides, coffeepot style, 7″ high, 5″ diameter base...........................35.00
UNION PACIFIC—Embossed on cap, teapot style, 6″ high, 5¼″ x 8″ oval base.............................20.00

Tallow pots

MISCELLANEOUS METALWARE

B&O—Cup, stamped on bottom, 2¾″ high, 3½″ diameter 6.00
C&NW RY—Flagman's case, 14½″ high, hinged lid, flag holder, "J-Urbana" 40.00

CB&Q RR CO—Watering can for depot flower garden, embossed in front, 2 rows of holes on top, handle and bail. "Johnson, Urbana, O".........................30.00
GN RY—Funnel, embossed, 6″ long, 4¼″ diameter...15.00

IC RR—Fire bucket, embossed, cone shaped, 13″ high, 14½″
    diameter, red, "Handlan" 35.00
MP LINES—Handled pitcher, embossed, 4″ tall, wide pouring
    lip 25.00*
NPR—Pail, emb. side, 10″ high, 12″ diameter top 30.00
NPR—Glue pot, stamped side, double boiler type, copper, 7½″
    high 55.00
StLSF RWY CO.—Water dipper, embossed on bottom, 8″ handle
    . . . . 30.00
SOO LINE—Coal scuttle, emb. at rear, 10½″ high 48.00
SOO LINE—Fire bucket, embossed, cone shaped, 19″ high,
    13½″ diameter, red, "J-Urbana" 45.00

MP Lines small tin pitcher

CAP BADGES, CAPS COMPLETE

The cap badge came in a number of styles, from plain rectangular panels to very ornate varieties. Most had black letters against a nickel-plated or gilt background. Others had raised letters and colored enamel work on contrasting backgrounds. Cap badges featuring an unusual occupation or one from an obscure or defunct railroad have a high value. Those not railroad marked, with titles only, such as "Dining Car Steward," "Sleeping Car Porter," "Conductor" or "Brakemen," are more moderately priced. Caution: Be on the lookout for repro's in the plain rectangular styles with black letters.

Many people collect the cap complete. This includes the badge, cap buttons and the gold or silver trim cord all intact. Value depends on the cap, badge, and trimmings all being original and having been kept in fine condition down through the years.

"AMTRAK TRAINMAN"—gold finish, rectangle, red/blue logo,
    black letters 21.50
"A.T.&S.F.R.R. BRAKEMAN"—nickel finish, plain rectangle
    . . . . 45.00
"BOSTON & MAINE AGENT"—gold finish, curved top
    . . . . 36.00
"BOSTON & MAINE BAGGAGE MASTER"—nickel finish,
    curved top 55.00
"BOSTON & MAINE CONDUCTOR"—gold finish, curved top
    . . . . 45.00
"BOSTON & MAINE STATION AGENT"—gold finish, curved
    top 40.00
"BOSTON & MAINE TRAINMAN"—nickel finish, curved top
    . . . . 38.00
"BUFFALO ROCHESTER AND PITTSBURGH AGENT"—gold
    finish, blue logo top 75.00
"BUFFALO ROCHESTER AND PITTSBURGH TRAINMAN"—
    silver finish, blue logo top 75.00
"C. & O. RY. CONDUCTOR"—embossed, pebbled gold
    background, curved top, milled border 35.00
"C. & O. RY. BRAKEMAN"—embossed, pebbled silver
    background, curved top, milled border 30.00
"C.B. & Q .R.R. CONDUCTOR"—nickel finish, plain rectangle
    . . . . 45.00
"C.G.W. RY. CONDUCTOR"—nickel finish, plain rect. . 75.00

"C.M.& St. P.AGENT"—embossed, pebbled silver background,
    fancy pointed top 35.00
"C.St.P.M.& O.RY. BRAKEMAN"—nickel finish, plain rectangle
    . . . . 60.00
"C.St.P.M. & O.RY. CONDUCTOR"—nickel finish, plain
    rectangle 65.00
"C. & N.W. RY. FREIGHT CONDUCTOR"—nickel finish, plain
    rectangle 50.00
"C.R.I. & P. BRAKEMAN"—embossed, pebbled silver
    background, curved top 27.50
"C.R.I. & P. CONDUCTOR"—embossed, pebbled gold
    background, curved top 32.50
"D.L. & W.RY. BRAKEMAN"—nickel finish, plain rectangle
    . . . . 50.00
"G.N. R.R. U.S. MAIL"—nickel finish, fancy pointed top 85.00
"G.N.RY. BRAKEMAN"—nickel finish, curved top 55.00
"G.N.RY. CONDUCTOR"—nickel finish, curved top . . .60.00
"GREAT NORTHERN RY. TRAIN SALESMAN"—nickel finish,
    fancy pointed top 95.00
"ILLINOIS CENTRAL PORTER"—raised, pebbled silver
    background, rectangle 25.00
"L.I.R.R. BRAKEMAN"—nickel finish, plain rectangle . 20.00
"L.I.R.R. CONDUCTOR"—nickel finish, plain rectangle 22.00
"L.S. & M.S. FREIGHT CONDUCTOR"—nickel finish, fancy
    pointed top 75.00

"MAINE CENTRAL TRAINMAN"—nickel finish, plain rectangle 25.00*

Rectangular-style cap badges

"M.C. R.R. CONDUCTOR"—embossed, pebbled gold background, "NEW YORK CENTRAL LINES" blue enamel oval, round top 40.00

"M. C.R.R. OPERATOR"—embossed, pebbled silver background, "NEW YORK CENTRAL LINES" blue enamel, oval, round top 40.00

"MILWAUKEE ROAD TRAINMAN"—raised, black rectangular background, logo above 20.00

"MINNESOTA & INTERNATIONAL AGENT"—moosehead in red and gold logo, top 150.00

"M & St.L RR AGENT"—nickel finish, plain rectangle 100.00

"M & St.L RR CONDUCTOR"—nickel finish, plain rectangle 100.00

"M & St.L RR CONDUCTOR"—gold on black enamel, logo at curved top 135.00

"M.St.P.& S.S.M.RY.CO.BAGGAGEMAN"—nickel finish, plain rectangle 47.50

"M.St.P.&S.S.M.RY.CO.CONDUCTOR"—nickel finish, plain rectangle 37.50

"M.St.P.& S.S.M.RY.CO. BRAKEMAN"—nickel finish, plain rectangle 35.00

"NEW YORK CENTRAL CONDUCTOR"—embossed, pebbled gold background, "NEW YORK CENTRAL LINES" blue enamel oval, round top 25.00*

"N.Y.N.H. & H. R.R. BAGGAGE MASTER"—nickel finish, fancy notched top 28.50

"N.Y.N.H. & H. R.R. TRAINMAN"—nickel finish, fancy notched top 25.00

"N.P. AGENT"—gold on black enamel, "NP" on monad logo at top 65.00

"NORTHERN PACIFIC RAILWAY BRAKEMAN"—nickel finish, plain rectangle 30.00

"NORTHERN PACIFIC RAILWAY CONDUCTOR"—nickel finish, plain rectangle 35.00

"NORTHERN PACIFIC RAILWAY FREIGHT CONDUCTOR"—nickel finish, plain rectangle 40.00

"P C CONDUCTOR"—red "PC" monogram on gold, curved top 25.00

"P R R CONDUCTOR"—red Keystone logo, title on pebbled gold background, ornate top 30.00

"P R R TRAINMAN"—red Keystone logo, title on pebbled gold background, ornate top 35.00

"P R R USHER"—red Keystone logo, title on pebbled gold background, ornate top 60.00*

Badges with enamelled and raised letters

"PULLMAN CONDUCTOR"—raised, pebbled gold background, rectangle 30.00

"PULLMAN PORTER"—raised, pebbled silver background, rectangle 30.00

"ROCK ISLAND BRAKEMAN"—logo on black enamel, raised title on silver background, arched top 30.00

"ROCK ISLAND CONDUCTOR"—logo on black enamel, raised title on gold background, arched top 35.00

"SANTA FE BRAKEMAN"—black logo, nickel finsh, fancy pointed top 40.00

"SANTA FE CONDUCTOR"—black logo, nickel finish, high curved top 45.00

"SOO LINE STATION AGENT"—nickel finish, fancy pointed top 65.00

"SOUTHERN RY. BRAKEMAN"—nickel finish, curved top 35.00

"SOUTHERN RY. CONDUCTOR"—nickel finish, curved top 37.50

"SOUTHERN RY. FLAGMAN"—nickel finish, curved top 60.00

"S.P. CONDUCTOR"-nickel finish, plain rectangle 25.00

"T.St.L.& K.C.R.R. BRAKEMAN"—nickel finish, curved top 75.00

"UNION PACIFIC BRAKEMAN"—raised, silver pebbled background, curved top, milled border 50.00

"UNION PACIFIC BRAKEMAN"—silver finish, plain rectangle 20.00

"UNION PACIFIC R.R. BRAKEMAN"—silver finish, plain rectangle 25.00

"UNION PACIFIC R.R. CONDUCTOR"—silver finish, plain rectangle 30.00
"UNION PACIFIC R.R. ELECTRICIAN"—gold finish, plain rectangle 40.00
"UNION PACIFIC R.R. ELECTRICIAN"—silver finish, plain rectangle 40.00
"UNION PACIFIC STATION AGENT"—raised, pebbled gold background, curved top, milled border 55.00

"UNION PACIFIC STATION BAGGAGE"—raised, pebbled gold background, curved top, milled border 55.00
"UNION PACIFIC R.R.TRUCKMAN"—nickel finish, plain rectangle 35.00*
"WABASH R.R. BRAKEMAN"—nickel finish, fancy notched top 38.00
"WABASH R.R. CONDUCTOR"—nickel finish, fancy notched top 42.00

NON-RAILROAD MARKED

"AGENT"—nickel finish, plain rectangle 10.00
"BAGGAGEMAN"—nickel finish, plain rectangle 12.00
"BRAKEMAN"—embossed, pebbled silver background, fancy pointed top 12.00
"CONDUCTOR"—gold finish, plain rectangle 10.00
"DINING CAR STEWARD"—gold finish, curved pointed top 15.00
"ENGINEER"—nickel finish, plain rectangle 20.00*
"FIREMAN"—nickel finish, plain rectangle 20.00
"SLEEPING CAR CONDUCTOR"—gold finish, curved pointed top 15.00
"SLEEPING CAR PORTER"—silver finish, curved pointed top 15.00
"TRAINMAN"—nickel finish, plain rectangle 10.00

Non-railroad marked, pin clasp type

TRAINMEN'S CAPS COMPLETE WITH BADGE AND TRIMMINGS

Assortment of caps with badges complete

"BOSTON & MAINE TRAINMAN"—nickel finish, curved top badge on deep blue wool cap 65.00
"C.M.St.P. & P. R.R. POLICE OFFICER"—nickel finish, ornate design, figures, eagle, shield and initials cut-out on indigo-dyed wool cap 125.00

"CONDUCTOR"—on gold braid band around black grosgrain cap 35.00
"GREAT NORTHERN RY. PORTER"—nickel finish, fancy pointed top badge on dark blue wool cap 75.00
"GREAT NORTHERN RY. TRAIN SALESMAN"—nickel finish, fancy pointed top badge on black grosgrain cap . . .175.00
"M.C.R.R. NEW YORK CENTRAL LINES CONDUCTOR"—raised letters on gold pebbled background, blue logo at top, badge on black grosgrain cap 85.00
"MILWAUKEE ROAD TRAINMAN"—silver letters on black enamel, red logo at top, badge on black grosgrain cap 65.00
"N.P. BRAKEMAN"—silver letters on black enamel, logo at top, badge on black grosgrain cap 75.00
"PULLMAN CONDUCTOR"—raised black letters on gold pebbled background, rectangular badge on black grosgrain cap 45.00
"SOO LINE BRAKEMAN"—raised letters on silver finished background, blue Soo Line logo on curved top, badge on black grosgrain cap 95.00
"SOUTHERN RY. CO. FLAGMAN"—nickel finish, curved top, badge on black grosgrain cap 85.00
"UNION PACIFIC R.R. BRAKEMAN"—rectangular badge on black grosgrain cap 55.00

CLOTH ITEMS

In addition to the table linens used in dining car service, a variety of other cloth items were in use over the years by the railroads, most of which are now being collected. This includes towels, pillow cases, sheets and sleeper blankets, coach car seat cover headrests, shop cloths or wiping rags, chef's caps, aprons, hot pad holders, etc. All of these bearing authentic railroad markings on them are being picked up, especially those from roads no longer in business which have become scarce and bring the higher prices. Condition plays an important part in determining value.

HAND TOWELS

AT&SF—Initials, "AT&SF RY.," 1951, on red center stripe, white, 13″ x 17″ 12.00

CMStP&P—Initials, "CMStP&P RR." stamped in black at bottom, 1956, white, 13½″ x 20½″ 10.00

GN—"GREAT NORTHERN" on one of two red stripes forming cross, undated, white, 18″ x 24″ 18.00

PULLMAN—"1914 PULLMAN-PULLMAN 1914" on one of two blue cross-stripes, white, 16″ x 26″ 22.00

PULLMAN—"1926 PULLMAN" on blue stripe, white, 17″ x 24″ 18.00

PULLMAN—"PROPERTY OF THE PULLMAN COMPANY," 1928, blue stripe, white, 17″ x 25″ 15.00

SOO LINE—"19 SOO LINE-SOO LINE 23" on two blue cross-stripes, white, 16″ x 20″ 25.00

Pullman hand towels

HEAD RESTS

ACL—"ATLANTIC COAST LINE RAILROAD, FLORIDA VACATIONLAND" at top (button-holes) sunbather beach scene and palms at bottom, 15″ x 18″ 7.50

CB&Q—Denver Zephyr with dome car and mountains pictured in brown at bottom edge on tan, 15″ x 18″ 8.00

C&NW—"The 400" at bottom, "NORTHWESTERN SYSTEM" at top, brown on tan, 15″ x 19½″ 8.00

CMStP&P—"THE MILWAUKEE ROAD" at buttonholes, logo and domeliners in script along bottom edge, brown on tan, 13″ x 18″ 12.50*

GN—"GREAT NORTHERN" and goat in orange at buttonholes on tan, 14″ x 19″ 9.50

IC—"ILLINOIS CENTRAL" in script at buttonholes, brown on tan, 15″ x 15½″ 6.00*

IC—Diamond logo at center, slipover double seat type, egg-shell white, grey logo, 40½″ x 14½″ 12.00

MStP&SSM—"SOO LINE" in red at buttonholes on beige, 15″ x 18″ 8.00

PRR—Logo and electric train in brown at bottom edge on tan, 15″ x 18″ 9.00

SR—Southern logo, "LOOK AHEAD-LOOK SOUTH" at buttonholes, green on pink, 15″ x 19″ 7.50

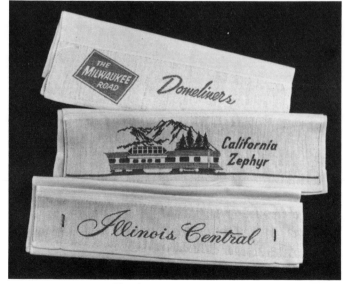

Head rest seat covers

UP—Winged streamliner motif at bottom, "U.P." at buttonholes, red-grey on yellow, 14″ x 19″ 5.00

SHOP CLOTHS

BURLINGTON ROUTE—Logo with repeated safety slogans, dark blue on beige, 16½″ x 17½″ 10.00
C&NW—Logo and "STAY ALERT, STAY ALIVE, SAFETY FIRST," repeated, blue on orange, 14″ x 17″ 8.00*
EJ&E RY—Logo and "SAFETY IS YOUR PERSONAL RESPONSIBILITY," repeated, blue on orange, 13½″ x 17½″15.00
IC—Diamond logo, "TAKE CARE, NOT CHANCES, THINK-WORK-LIVE-SAFELY," repeated, blue on white, 18″ x 30″ 7.50
MILWAUKEE ROAD—Logo and "WORK SAFELY, WIPE OUT ACCIDENTS" in blue on tan, 14″ x 17″ 4.00
ROCK ISLAND—Logo, "DON'T GET HURT, LOOK-THINK-BE ALERT" repeated, blue on yellow, 13″ x 16″ 5.00*

Shop cloths

BLANKETS

Sleeping car blanket

PULLMAN—Wool, pink shade with darker "THE PULLMAN CO." logo at center 65.00
GREAT NORTHERN—Wool, rose color with brown goat silhouette logo at center 75.00
GREAT NORTHERN—Wool, brown and tan checkered with "GREAT NORTHERN RAILWAY" rectangle logo at center 150.00*
SOO LINE—Wool, brown and beige squares and bands with old style Banner logo at center .150.00
SOO LINE—Wool, gray and tan squares w/black lines and bands, later style canted box logo at center 100.00
UNION PACIFIC—Wool, grey, with black "THE OVERLAND ROUTE" shield logo at center 125.00

PILLOW CASES

BN—"PILLOW RENTAL 50¢ TO DESTINATION ON BURLINGTON NORTHERN" stamped in black on white, standard size 8.00
BURLINGTON ROUTE—Logo stenciled in black, standard size 6.00
CMStP&P—Initials stenciled in black, standard size 8.00
PULLMAN—"PROPERTY OF THE PULLMAN CO." (logo) stamped in black on white, standard size 4.00*
UP—Shield logo stamped near open end, white, standard size 5.00
UP—"CITY OF SAN FRANCISCO," orange letters in center strip, white, standard size 10.00
UPRR—"CHAIR CAR" stamped in black on white, standard size 5.00*

Bedding - sheet and pillow cases

SHEETS

SR—"Serves The South" logo, "LOOK AHEAD, LOOK SOUTH, SOUTHERN RAILWAY SYSTEM" stamped in green on white, 81″ x 64″.................................14.00*

UP—Shield logo repeatedly stamped, white, 81″ x 64″. 10.00
GN RY—repeatedly stamped, white, 81″ x 64″.......12.00

MISCELLANEOUS CLOTH ITEMS

C&O—Bath towel, "CHESAPEAKE & OHIO RAILWAY" across center, blue letters on white, 22″ x 38″..........20.00
CNS&M—Cotton money sack, "RETURN TO CHICAGO NORTH SHORE & MILWAUKEE RR CO. HIGHWOOD, ILL. $500.00" in black on white, 8½″ x 14″.........15.00
CStPM&O—Cotton money sack, "CHICAGO, ST. PAUL, MINNEAPOLIS & OMAHA RAILWY CO. ST. PAUL" stamped in black on white, 5½″ x 10″..................18.00
IC—Dish towel, with IC logo & safety slogans, blue, white 8.00
NP—Hot pad holder, monad logo, "SAFETY AT WORK, SAFETY AT HOME" red checkered border, 6″ x 6″....15.00*
NP—Felt pennant, Yellowstone Park Line logo, "NORTHERN PACIFIC RWY," red, black & white printing on blue, 28″ long 30.00
RY EX—Cotton money sack, "PROPERTY OF RY EX AGY No. 912843" stamped in black on white..............4.00
SANTA FE—Chef's cap, logo and "DC" stamped in black on white 22.00

Hot pad holder

DATE NAILS

Date nails are small nails with the year date raised or indented into the nailhead. Date nails were pounded into the tie when it was laid in the roadbed, remaining visible for research purposes. Those prior to 1910 bear only a single digit, such as 6, 7, 8, or two digits, as 02, 05, 07; after that time, the last two numbers of the year were shown. Most of these nails came in steel, but copper, aluminum, and even plastic date nails were made. The heads usually were round, but other shapes can be found. Shanks vary in length. Collecting date nails and classifying them covers a broad field. Some collectors simply try to see how many different types and dates they can find.

The Texas Date Nail Collectors Association, Lufkin, Texas, is a good source from which to buy, sell or trade date nails through the mail. Several books, available in retail book stores, have been published on the hobby. A brief listing of date nails representing railroads in the Minneapolis-St. Paul area is shown here.

Raised and indent digits

C&NW—Steel, square head, "7" indented, stubby, 1¾″..2.00
C&NW—Steel, round head, "11" indented, stubby, 1¾″..5.00
C&NW—Steel, round head, "27" indented...........1.00*
GN RR—Steel, round head, "07" indented...........5.00
GN RR—Steel, round head, "09" indented...........3.00
GN RR—Steel, round head, "T7" indented, letter T.....5.00
GN RR—Steel, round head, "25" raised..............1.00
GN RR—Steel, round head, "31" raised..............50¢
IC—Steel, square head, "24" raised.................4.00

Date nails

MILW. ROAD—Steel, round head, "30" raised . . . . .50¢
MILW. ROAD—Steel, round head, "34" raised . . . . .50¢
MILW. ROAD—Copper, round head, "27" indented, small,
    1½" 2.00
MILW. ROAD—Copper, round head, "39" indented, small,
    1½" 2.00
MN&S RY—Steel, round head, "35" raised 3.00
NP—Steel, round head, "11" indented 2.00
NP—Steel, round head, "17" indented 2.00
NP—Steel, square head, "27" raised, square shank 1.00*
NP—Steel, round head, "32" raised . . . . .50¢
ROCK ISLAND—Steel, round head, "29" raised . . . . .50¢
SOO LINE—Steel, round head, "36" raised . . . . .50¢

DINING CAR COLLECTIBLES

Dining car collectibles include china, silver, glassware, menus, linens and the miscellany of items used in the club car.

Most railroads featured their own exclusive designs on their china, although others used a stock pattern. The railroad's logo, name, or initials appeared on the topside, or they were backstamped, along with the manufacturer's name. There is a great variety of patterns and pieces to be found; the earlier patterns or pieces from short-lived railroads, commanding premium prices. The two popular steam and diesel service plates from the Missouri Pacific, the complete set of Illinois Central's French Quarter service plates, and the Chesapeake & Ohio's famous George Washington service plate, bring very high prices. All railroad china must be in perfect condition to warrant the prices listed here.

Silver holloware consists of the various serving pieces, such as coffee pots, sugar and creamers, cake stands, compotes, bread trays, and the like. These have the railroad's initials or logos on the topside or are railroad-marked on the bottom, along with the maker's name. Many pieces are both top and bottom marked, and these are especially desirable. The earlier pieces were usually quite ornate, while those from the years of the popular "name trains" are more streamlined.

There was a great variety of knives, forks and spoons used on dining car table settings. These are known as flatware. They, too, came top or bottom marked, or were double marked and made in a number of patterns. All silverware must be in perfect condition to bring top price. The earlier pieces and those from defunct roads have the higher value.

Tumblers, cocktail sets, wine glasses, water pitchers, and other railroad-marked glassware are being collected. The more unusual pieces, such as cruets, or cut glass syrup pitchers, are not easily found and are priced high. Most pieces available today are the miscellaneous tumblers and various bar items. Damaged glassware has little or no value.

Dining car menus are much in demand today. Many of them featured very attractive covers; others were quite plain. The early menus have the higher value. Some menus were in the shape of a special food item the railroad featured in their dining car, as NP's Wenatchee baked apple or famous Idaho baked potato. These unusually shaped menus are especially desirable. Pristine condition is an important factor in pricing.

The tablecloths and napkins used on the dining cars of yesteryear are now being collected. These were usually white, although later on some came in various pastel shades. Many had the railroad's logo stamped on them, while others had their name or initials woven into the material. Linens showing wear or stains are priced lower.

The miscellaneous stir sticks used in the club car are also now being picked up along with coasters, paper napkins, toothpicks, and such—all railroad-marked, of course.

CHINA

China pieces are listed by Railroad, then pattern name and description. More extensive pattern information may be found in Richard Luckin's dining car china book *Dining On Rails*.

KEY TO CHINA MANUFACTURERS

BSHR:—Bauscher
BUFF:—Buffalo
IRQ:—Iroquois
LAMB:—Lamberton
LEX:—Lenox
LIM:—Limoges
MAD:—Maddock (N.J.)
MDK:—Maddock (Eng.)

MIN:—Minton
MYR:—Mayer
R-D:—Royal Doulton
SCM:—Scammell
SGO:—Shenango
STR:—Sterling
SYR:—Syracuse
WAR:—Warwick

KEY TO ABBREVIATIONS

BS:—Backstamped
NBS:—Not backstamped
TM:—Top marked
SM:—Side marked

ACL—"Carolina"—grey pinstripe border, 9″ dinner plate, BS, STR 35.00
ACL—"Palmetto"—logo, green leaves, 9″ dinner plate, TM, NBS, WAR 175.00
ALASKA—"McKinley"—Mt. McKinley logo, 5¾″ plate, TM, NBS, SGO 200.00
AT&SF—"Mimbreno"—flying bird, 2″ butter pat, BS, SYR
. . . . 40.00*

Butter pats

AT&SF—"California Poppy"—yellow poppies, cup & saucer, NBS, SYR 35.00
AT&SF—"Griffon"—mythical lion-eagle border design, 9″ dinner plate, BS, BSHR 225.00
AT&SF—"Bleeding Blue"—blue letters & stripes, 12¼″ x 5¾″ celery, TM, NBS, SCM 150.00

B&O—"Centennary"—Lord Baltimore locomotive in border, 9″ dinner plate, BS, SCM 75.00
B&O—"Centennary"—diesel-electric #51 locomotive, 10½″ dinner plate, BS, LAMB 45.00
B&O—"Centennary"—Cincinnatian in border, 10½″ dinner plate, BS, SGO 35.00
B&O—"Capitol"—gold Capitol logo, 6¼″ bowl, TM, NBS, WAR 35.00
B&O—"Derby"—blue flower design center, 9″ dinner plate, NBS, SGO 65.00
B&A—"Berkshire"—double logo "Boston & Albany-New York Central Lines," 3½″ pedestal compote, TM, NBS . . 200.00
CN—"Maritime"—maple leaf logo, 5¼″ x 4″ oval sauce, BS, Haviland 85.00
CP—"Maple Leaf Blue"—blue maple leaf border design, 9″ dinner plate, TM, NBS, MIN 28.00
CP—"Maple Leaf Brown"—brown maple leaf border design, 5¾″ x 9″ soup plate, TM, NBS, LIM 32.00
C&O—"George Washington"—Geo. Washington portrait, wide gold border, 10½″ service plate, BS, BUFF 700.00
C&O—"George Washington"—small oval portrait top, 6½″ x 9¼″ oval dish, BS, SYR 200.00
C&O—"Chessie"—Chessie kitten logo, 9¾″ dinner plate, TM, NBS, SYR 80.00
C&O—"Train Ferry Service"—boat logo, 9½″ divided dinner plate, NBS, SYR 75.00
C&NW—"Flambeau"—pinstripes, 3″ double egg cup, NBS, SGO
. . . . 25.00
C&NW—"Patriot"—red/blue bars, red pinstripe border, 9″ dinner plate, BS, SGO 85.00
C&NW—"400"—400 diesel streamliner, 10½″ service plate, BS, SGO 550.00

CB&Q—"Violets & Daisies"—loose flowers, 5¾" plate, BS, BUFF
....28.00
CB&Q—"Aristocrat"—Burlington Route logo, 7¼" plate, NBS,
SYR 85.00
CB&Q—"Chuck Wagon"—"The Chuck Wagon C-DZ," bouillon
cup, SM, NBS, SYR...........................85.00
CB&Q—China teapot, gold logo on blue, Hall's.......95.00
CI&L—"Monon"—M logo in center circle, 6¼" plate, TM, NBS,
SGO 135.00
CMStP&P—"Peacock"—colorful peacock motif, 3" double egg
cup, NBS, SYR...........................18.00
CMStP&P—"Traveler"—flying geese, demitasse cup and saucer,
BS, SYR 75.00*

Cups and saucers - coffee and demitasse

CMStP&P—"Olympian"—gold logo cup, Olympian on saucer, cup
and saucer set, NBS, LEX....................125.00
CMStP&P—"Galatea"—classical design, 9¾" x 4½" celery dish,
NBS, SYR 85.00
CRI&P—"LaSalle"—RI monogram in green border design, 5¾"
x 8¼" oval dish, NBS, BUFF.................125.00
CRI&P—"Golden Rocket"—red-orange logo w/band, 7¼" plate,
NBS, SGO 135.00
CRI&P—"Golden State"—floral and oranges, 7¼" plate, BS,
BUFF 175.00
D&H—"Adirondack"—D&H diesel freight and canal, 10½" plate,
TM, NBS, SYR...........................100.00
D&IR—"Vermillion"—Indian logo, Vermillion Route, 9" dinner
plate, NBS, SYR...........................150.00
D&RGW—"Prospector"—"Rio Grande," 6¾" salad bowl, TM,
NBS, SYR 45.00
DL&W—"St. Albans"—floral pattern spaced in border, 8½" plate,
NBS, SYR 65.00
ERIE—"Starucca"—Erie diamond logo, blue pinstripe border,
5¾" bowl, NBS, IRQ.......................48.00
ERIE—"Susquehana"—Erie diamond logo, floral design border,
9¾" x 5" celery dish, TM, BS, BUFF............75.00
ERIE—"Gould"—Erie in script, floral border, 8¾" x 5⅞ plat-
ter, TM, NBS, SGO........................275.00
FEC—"Carolina"—logo and stripes, 10¼" dinner plate, BS, STR
.... 100.00
GN—"Mountains & Flowers"—mountains background, flowers
foreground, 6½" plate, BS, SYR.............40.00

GN—"Glory Of The West"—mountains and pine trees, demitasse
cup & saucer, BS, SYR.....................150.00*
GN—"Rocky"—colorful animal characters, mountain goat logo,
5" cereal bowl, SM NBS, SYR..................150.00
GN—"Hill"—GN monogrammed initials, 4¾" x 6¼" oval dish,
NBS, Greenwood China.....................65.00
GN—"Glacier"—multi-floral center, pinstripes, 9¾" dinner plate,
BS, BSHR..............................350.00
GN—"Oriental"—flower pot design border, cup & saucer, BS,
SYR 200.00*
IC—"French Quarter"—Old Grima Home, 10⅝" service plate,
BS, BSHR...............................350.00
IC—"Coral"—pink/white floral, 7¼" plate, NBS, SYR . . 22.00
IC—"Pirate"—pirate and palms border, 10" service plate, NBS,
SYR 150.00
MStP&SSM—"Citation"—banner Soo Line logo, 2" butter pat,
NBS, MDK..............................50.00*
MStP&SSM—"Logan"—flower design around border, 9" dinner
plate, BS, MYR...........................175.00
MStP&SSM—"Citation"—banner Soo Line logo, 5½" x 7¾" oval
dish, NBS, MDK...........................85.00
MKT—"Blue Bonnet"—2 flowers at lower border, 9¾" dinner
plate, BS, BUFF..........................225.00
MKT—"Old Abbey"—Alamo in center, 10½" service plate, BS,
BUFF 550.00
MOPAC—"Eagle"—The Eagle motif, 5½" plate, TM, NBS, SYR
...............................35.00
MOPAC—"State Flowers"—steam train center, 10½" service
plate, TM, NBS, SYR......................225.00
MOPAC—"State Capitols"—diesel streamliner center, 10½" ser-
vice plate, TM, BS, SYR....................350.00
N&W—"Cavalier"—"N&W Ry" script in floral border, 7" salad
bowl, TM, NBS, LAMB......................75.00
N&W—"Bristol"—monogram logo in floral wreath, 7¼" x 5½"
oval baker, TM, NBS, SYR..................110.00
NYC—"Country Gardens"—brown garden scene center, 11" ser-
vice plate, NBS, BUFF.....................65.00
NYC—"DeWitt Clinton"—DeWitt Clinton engine 1831 in border,
9" dinner plate, TM, BS, BUFF.............50.00
NYC—"DePew"—delicate floral motif, 6" au gratin dish, BS,
Haviland 75.00
NYC—"Mercury"—NYC in 12 vertical lines, 9" dinner plate, TM,
NBS, SYR..............................45.00
NYC—"Mohawk"—NYC in black stripes on pink, 10" dinner
plate, TM, NBS, SYR......................100.00
NYC—"Vanderbilt"—geometric border design, 8½" x 5¾" plat-
ter, BS, BUFF............................50.00
NYC—"Hyde Park"—pink/green floral pattern, 7¼" x 10¾" plat-
ter, BS, LIM............................125.00
NYC&StL—"Bellevue"—logo & stripes, 9¾" dinner plate, TM,
NBS, Walker............................150.00
NYNH&H—"Platinum Blue"—nude kneeling figure, sauce boat,
BS, BUFF................................55.00
NYNH&H—"Merchants"—steam train, map & ship, 8¾" dinner
plate, TM, BS, BUFF......................85.00
NYNH&H—"Indian Tree"—floral & geometric, 5" sauce boat,
BS, SGO.................................55.00*

Sauce boats

NP—"Monad"—Monad logo, 9″ dinner plate, TM, NBS, SGO
. . . . 85.00

NP—"Yellowstone"—Yellowstone Park Line logo, 9″ dinner plate,
TM, NBS, SGO 125.00

NP—"Garnet"—green & purple leaf border, 4½″ x 6″ oval dish,
BS, MYR 85.00

PRR—"Broadway"—pinstripes & cross-hatched border, 8″ plate,
TM, BS, MYR 38.00

PRR—"Purple Laurel"—pinstripe & floral border design, 11″ x
7¾″ platter, BS, STR 32.00

PRR—"Keystone"—Keystone logo, brown pinstripes, 4⅜″ x 9″
oval dish, TM, NBS, WAR 35.00

PRR—"Mountain Laurel"—green border, floral spray center, 9¼″
plate, BS, SGO 35.00

PULLMAN—"Indian Tree"—Indian tree center, floral & geometric
border, 8¼″ x 5¾″ platter, TM, NBS, SYR 95.00

PULLMAN—"Calumet"—Pullman name w/pinstripes, 6¼″ plate,
TM, NBS, SYR 50.00

READING—"Stotesbury"—ornate border design, 4¼″ x 10″
celery dish, BS, LAMB 150.00

SD&A—"Carriso"—logo in brown pinstripe border, 9″ dinner
plate, TM, NBS, BUFF 200.00

StL&SF—"Denmark"—blue leaf design, 9¾″ dinner plate, NBS,
SYR 75.00

SAL—"Palm Beach"—"Seaboard" w/floral border, 4½″ x 10″
celery dish, TM, NBS, SYR 125.00

SP—"Harriman Blue"—old Sunset logo, wavy blue border, cup
only, SM, NBS, MAD 95.00

SP—"Sunset"—new Sunset logo, green floral border, cup, NBS,
SYR, SM 65.00

SP—"Prairie Mountains Wild Flowers"—various mountain wild
flowers, 9½″ dinner plate, BS, SYR 75.00

SP—"Sunset"—Sunset logo, green floral border, 10¼″ dinner
plate, TM, BS, BUFF 150.00

SR—"Peach Blossom"—SR logo in pinstripe border, 7¼″ plate,
TM, NBS, BUFF 135.00

SR—"Piedmont"—blue-green pinstripes, demitasse cup & saucer,
BS, STR 40.00

UP—"Harriman Blue"—wavy blue border, 5½″ x 12″ celery dish,
BS, SCM 55.00

UP—"Winged Streamliner"—winged streamliner motif, demitasse
cup & saucer, TM, NBS, STR 35.00

UP—"Overland"—shield logo, miniature western scenes in border,
7¼″ x 3½″ pickle dish, TM, BS, SGO 85.00

UP—"Challenger"—"The Challenger," 6½″ plate, TM, NBS, SYR
. . . . 40.00

UP—"Desert Flower"—green shading, scalloped edge, 9″ bowl,
BS, SYR 30.00

WAB—"Banner"—Flag logo, 5½″ plate, TM, NBS, SYR
. . . . 100.00

WP—"Feather River"—"Feather River Route," red feather design,
5½″ plate, TM, NBS, SGO 55.00

SILVER HOLLOWARE   See Everett Maffett's book *Silver Banquet* for year marks.

KEY TO ABBREVIATIONS

BM—Bottom marked
SM—Side marked
TM—Top marked
HH—Hollow handle

SILVER MANUFACTURERS

GOR—Gorham
INT'L—International
MER—Meriden
R&B—Reed & Barton
ROG—Rogers
WAL—Wallace

ACL—covered sugar, 8 oz., BM "ACL," MER 85.00

B&M RR—covered sugar, 6 oz., BM "B&M RR," MER
. . . . 95.00

C&EI—creamer w/hinged lid, 2-line finial, 8 oz., BM "C&EI RR,"
R&B 45.00

C&NW RY—Coffee pot, 14 oz. winged finial, BM "C&NW RY"
script, INT'L 95.00

CM&StP—bowl, 5″ diameter, ornate border design, BM
"CM&StP" script, R&B 125.00

CStPM&O RY—footed toothpick holder, 3¼″ high, BM
"CStPM&O RY" script, R&B 100.00

DM&NR—creamer, ¼ pt., SM "DM&N RY" script, MER (rare)
. . . . 150.00

GN—coffee pot, 14 oz., BM "Great Northern Ry.", INT'L
. . . . 75.00

GN—syrup w/attached drip tray, BM "Great Northern Ry," INT'L
. . . . 125.00

GN—footed cakestand, beaded lattice edging, BM "Great Northern Ry," MER 225.00

GN—coffee pot, 8 oz., beaded edging, SM "GNR" fancy
monogram, BM "Great Northern Ry .," MER 150.00

GN—butter chip, 3½″ diameter, TM "GN," BM "Great Northern Ry.", INT'L 30.00
GM&O—water pitcher, 4 pt., hinged cover, BM "GM&O," INT'L 185.00
ICRR—covered sugar, 6 oz. SM "ICRR" fancy monogram, INT'L 150.00
ICRR—mustard pot, hinged lid w/hole for spoon, SM "ICRR" script, GOR 75.00
LACKAWANNA—covered sugar, 8 oz., BM "Lackawanna," INT'L 125.00
L&N—sauce boat, BM "L&N," INT'L 75.00
NYC LINES—covered sugar, 8 oz., BM "NYC LINES," R&B75.00
NPR—coffee pot, 1 pt., ornate gooseneck, SM logo, BM "NPR," R&B 185.00*

Holloware

NPR—sugar & creamer, pair, Pagoda style, SM logo, BM "NPR," R&B 350.00*
NPR—bouillon cup holder, BM "Northern Pacific Railway Co.," INT'L 65.00
NP RY—crumb scraper 12¼″ long, BM "NP RY" script, 1847 ROG 65.00
PRR—ice bowl, SM Keystone logo, INT'L 75.00
ROCK ISLAND LINES—ice cream shell w/3 ball feet, BS "Rock Island Lines," WAL 55.00
ROCK ISLAND LINES—hot cake cover, 6 air holes, finial top, BS "Rock Island Lines," GOR 65.00
SOO LINE—soda bottle holder, TM banner logo, GOR 95.00
SOO LINE—bread tray, 13¼″ x 6″, TM banner logo, GOR 135.00
SOO LINE—coffee pot, ⅞ pt., goose neck, SM banner logo, GOR 175.00
SOO LINE—coffee pot, 8 oz., BM "Soo Line," R&B . .85.00
SOUTHERN PACIFIC—change tray, passenger train across center, BM "Southern Pacific," script, R&B 150.00
SOUTHERN PACIFIC—pair salt & peppers, SM winged logo, BM "Southern Pacific," script, INT'L 95.00
UPRR—menu stand w/2 pencil holders, BM "UPRR" script, INT'L 65.00
UPRR—butter pat, BM "UPRR," INT'L 30.00
WABASH—covered sugar, 14 oz., SM ornate "W," BM "Wabash," R&B 120.00

SILVER FLATWARE

Flatware pieces are listed by Railroad, then by Pattern Name. More extensive pattern information may be found in Dominy & Morganfruh's *A Collector's Guide To Railroad Flatware.*

AT&SF RY—Cromwell, demitasse spoon, TM "AT&SF RY," INT'L 28.00
SANTA FE—Albany, teaspoon, BM "Santa Fe," GOR .22.00
ACL—Zephyr, bouillon spoon, TM "ACL," INT'L 20.00
B&O—Cromwell, teaspoon, TM "B&O" script, R&B . . .25.00
C&NW RY—Modern Art, dinner knife, BM "C&NW RY" script, R&B 25.00
CCC&StL RY—Alden, teaspoon, TM "CCC&StL RY," R&B 30.00
CGW RY—Clarendon, teaspoon, TM "CGW RY" script, R&B 35.00
CMStP&P RR—Broadway, soup spoon, BM "CMStP&P RR," INT'L 15.00
CStPM&O RY—Modern Art, dinner knife, BM "CStPM&O Ry" script, R&B 25.00
D&H—Royal, dinner knife, TM "The D&H," R&B 30.00
D&RGW RR—Belmont, teaspoon, TM "D&RGW RR," R&B 25.00
ERIE—Elmwood, soup spoon, TM logo, GOR 28.00
FEC RY—Cromwell, oyster fork, TM "FEC RY," INT'L 18.00
GM&O—Broadway, dinner fork, TM "GM&O," INT'L . .18.00
GN—Hutton, demitasse spoon, TM "GN," INT'L 20.00

Flatware pieces

GN—Hutton, dinner fork, TM "GN," INT'L 16.00
GN—Hutton, dinner knife, TM "GN," INT'L 17.00
GN—Hutton, tablespoon, TM "GN," INT'L 15.00
GN—Hutton, teaspoon, TM "GN," INT'L 14.00
ICRR—Alden, teaspoon, TM ornate monogram, R&B . .18.00

LACKAWANNA—Cromwell, iced teaspoon, TM "Lackawanna," INT'L 25.00

NC&StL—Sierra, dinner fork, BM "NC&StL," R&B . . . 28.00

NYC—Century, dessert fork, BM "NYC," INT'L 15.00

NYC—Century, grapefruit spoon, BM "NYC," INT'L . . . 18.00

NYC—Century, iced teaspoon, BM "NYC," INT'L 20.00

NPR—Alden, dinner fork, TM logo, R&B 25.00

NPR—Alden, soup spoon, TM logo, R&B 22.00

NPR—Winthrop, dinner knife, ornate handle, TM "NPR" script, GOR 26.00

NPR—Winthrop, iced teaspoon, TM "NPR" script, GOR 30.00

NORTHERN PACIFIC RAILWAY COMPANY—Silhouette, butter knife, BM full name, INT'L 20.00

PRR—Kings Alternate, dessert fork, TM Keystone logo, INT'L 28.00

PULLMAN—Roosevelt, tablespoon, BM "Pullman," INT'L 20.00

ROCK ISLAND LINES—Albany, dinner fork, TM "RI" monogram, INT'L 18.00

SEABOARD—Albany, butter knife, TM "Seaboard," INT'L 18.00

SEABOARD—Albany, grapefruit spoon, TM "Seaboard," INT'L 15.00

SEABOARD—Albany, pickle fork, TM "Seaboard," INT'L 18.00

SOO LINE—Sussex, iced teaspoon, TM logo, INT'L . . . 35.00

SOO LINE—Sussex, tablespoon, TM logo, INT'L 30.00

SOUTHERN—Sierra, sugar tongs, SM "Southern," R&B 35.00

S.P.CO.—Westfield, teaspoon, TM "S.P.CO." script, MER 18.00

SOUTHERN PACIFIC—Broadway, dinner fork, BM "Southern Pacific" script, INT'L 18.00

SOUTHERN PACIFIC—Broadway, teaspoon, BM "Southern Pacific" script, INT'L 16.00

SP&S RY—Embassy, dinner knife, BM "SP&S RY," R&B 30.00

SP&S RY—Embassy, soup spoon, BM "SP&S RY," R&B 30.00

UPRR—Zephyr, oyster fork, BM "UPRR" script, INT'L 25.00

UPRR—Zephyr, teaspoon, BM "UPRR" script, INT'L . . 20.00

WESTERN PACIFIC—Hutton, tablespoon, BM logo, INT'L 16.00

GLASSWARE, GLASSWARE WITH SILVER COMPONENTS

BN—mug, clear, "BN Burlington Northern" green, "Transportation Needs You" 1972, black 9.50

C&O—tumbler, "C&O For Progress," in blue 8.00

CN—sherbet, cut glass stem, pinched sides, "Canadian National Railways," frosted logo on side 35.00

D&H—water glass, thick bottom, "The D&H" etched old style logo 25.00

FRISCO—tumbler, Frisco logo in blue 6.00

GN—caster stand w/2 cruets, SM "GN," BM "Great Northern Ry.," INT'L 175.00*

GN—cruet, clear glass, etched Great Northern Railway goat logo 100.00

GN—cruet, clear glass, frosted older goat logo 150.00

IC—wine glass, stemmed, clear, frosted IC diamond logo 15.00

M&StLRR—water bottle in silver frame, BM lid "M&StLRR," R&B 350.00

IC—old fashion glass, large w/train 6.00

MOPAC—milk bottle, ½ pint, Missouri Pacific buzz-saw logo one side, "Sunnymeade Farm. Bismarck, Mo." other side . 7.50

MOPAC—milk bottle, quart, buzz-saw logo, clear 20.00

NP—cordial, 3¾", etched Yellowstone Park logo 25.00*

Glass/silver - condiment bottles in silver stand

Glassware - cordials

NP—water glass, black and red Monad logo..........8.00
NP—pair salt & peppers, clear glass, ornate silver tops marked "No. Pac. Ry.".....................................50.00
NP—milk bottle, ½ pint, embossed "Northern Pacific Railway, Dairy and Poultry Farm, Kent, Wn."..............35.00
NYC SYSTEM—stemmed cordial, 4¼″, gold New York Central System logo.................................10.00
PRR—high ball glass, large, w/red Keystone and diesel locomotive 15.00

ROCK ISLAND LINES—caster stand, 3 glass shakers, BM "Rock Island Lines" INT'L.........................125.00
SANTA FE—tumbler, clear, etched "Santa Fe" in script.5.00
SOO LINE—syrup, cut glass, silver handle and lid marked "Soo Line"..175.00
UP—shot glass, clear, etched Union Pacific shield logo..5.50
UP—tumbler, clear, frosted Union Pacific shield logo...6.50
UP—cocktail set, mixer, 4 glasses, clear, frosted Union Pacific shield logo on each..........................30.00

MENUS

AMTRAK—"Good Morning" club breakfast, single card, 7″ x 11″, recent...1.00
AT&SF—"The Chief," dinner, 1939, red monogram on cover 5.50
AT&SF—"The Grand Canyon Ltd.," luncheon, 1940, gold monogram on cover.........................6.00
BURLINGTON ROUTE—"Zephyr," luncheon, 1943, Zephyr streamliner cover............................5.50
CANADIAN PACIFIC—"The Dominion," dinner, 1952, Peggy Cove scene cover..........................5.00
C&NW—"400," dinner, Dec. 1954, "Season's Greetings," pioneer locomotive scene on cover.............6.50
C&NW—"Northwestern Limited," supper and wine list, Sept. '05, football player on cover......................25.00
C&NW—"Famous Trains," supper, with today's special insert page, 12-1-09, couple seated at table on cover.....35.00
GREAT NORTHERN—"Empire Builder," breakfast, 1936, "Riding Black Horse," Indian chief on cover, colorful 22.50
FRED HARVEY—Union Terminal, Cleveland, dinner, June 20, 1939, 1876 dining table scene on cover...........4.50
ILLINOIS CENTRAL—"Centennial" luncheon, single card, 8″ x 11″, Centennial medallion 1851-1951 depicted upper right 4.00
ILLINOIS CENTRAL—"Panama Limited," breakfast, 1963, transition of locomotives, Iron Horse to modern diesel...4.00
LEHIGH VALLEY—"Black Diamond Express," dinner, 1927, chef and Black Diamond Express on cover........30.00

MILWAUKEE ROAD—"The Hiawatha," luncheon, 1962, Thunderbird design on cover....................5.00
NEW YORK CENTRAL—"Empire State Express," luncheon, 1939, new streamlined 20th Century Ltd. on cover...7.50
NP—Special excursion, St. Paul Jobber's Union, dinner and wine list, 1885, litho. of Indian maiden front cover, dining car back cover, (rare).........................75.00
NP—Casserole shape, 4 pages, luncheon, 1911, dining car table setting on back cover.......................30.00
NP—Apple shape, 4 pages, breakfast, 1914, dining car table setting on back cover.........................25.00
NP—Baked potato shape, 4 pages, dinner, 1914, dining car kitchen scene on back cover.....................35.00
ROCK ISLAND—"Route Of The Rockets," luncheon, Dec. 1945, red Rocket and steam locomotive on cover, holly sprig 7.50
SEABOARD—breakfast, 1943, WWII, flag and soldier blowing bugle on cover..............................6.00
SOUTHERN PACIFIC—special "Anzar Temple Pilgrimage," luncheon, June, 1926, couple seated at dining car table 30.00
UNION PACIFIC—"Domeliner," City Of Los Angeles, breakfast, 1971, Fremont St., Las Vegas, on cover...........2.00
WESTERN PACIFIC-RIO GRANDE-BURLINGTON—Chicago Democratic Convention, 2 pages, July 10, 1940, cartoon characters of donkey and bear on cover. Tied with red/white/blue ribbon........................22.50

TABLECLOTHS

BALTIMORE & OHIO—Capitol logo center, floral design border woven in, white on white, 34″ x 34″............20.00
BURLINGTON ROUTE—logo stamped in black near edge, white, 35″ x 35″.....................................22.50
C&NW—Chicago Northwestern Line logo and "CStPM&O RY" below, overall fleur-de-lis design woven in, white on white, 54″ x 68″...75.00

ROCK ISLAND—large logo at center, floral design around, woven in, white on white, 34″ x 33″..................35.00
SOO LINE—logo at center, woven in, white on white, 34″ x 34″ 42.50
UNION PACIFIC—"UP RR" woven small near edge, roses woven in, rose pink, 50″ x 42″.....................18.00

NAPKINS

BURLINGTON ROUTE—logo at center woven in, white on white, 18½″ x 21″................................10.00

C&NW—Chicago & Northwestern Line logo at center, floral border design woven in, white on white, 22″ x 22″.15.00

FRISCO LINES—name woven into fancy floral design each corner, white on white, 22″ x 20½″ 22.00

GREAT NORTHERN RY—logo at center, woven in, white on white, 22″ x 21″ 12.00

MILWAUKEE ROAD—Hiawatha emblem printed in corner, plain border, magenta on tan, 10¾″ x 16½″ 15.00

NORTHERN PACIFIC RY—Monad logo at center, plain border, woven in, red/white on tan, 20″ x 21″ 10.00

NORTHERN PACIFIC RY—Yellowstone Park Line logo at center, woven in, red/brown on tan, 13″ x 18″ 18.00

SOUTHERN PACIFIC LINES—Sunset logo at center, fancy border with poppies woven in, white on white, 21″ x 21″ 25.00

UNION PACIFIC—"UP RR" woven small near edge, rose pink, 19½″ x 20½″ 6.00

STIR STICKS

AMTRAK—plastic, blue, arrow top 1.00*

B&O—iron, in form of golf club 12.50

BURLINGTON ROUTE—plastic, blue, dome car cut-out 7.50*

C&NW-plastic, white, "Route of the 400." spoon tip 5.00*

GN—plastic, "Empire Builder," goat at top 8.00*

GN—plastic, red, "Western Star," goat at top 5.00

GN—plastic, "The Growing Great Northern," modern goat 4.00

GN—plastic, "From Ranch of Empire Builder" on rod . . 2.00

GN—plastic, ball top, "Great Northern Railway" on rod . 1.50

HIAWATHA—"Nothing finer on rails," clear glass, spoon tip 15.00*

SP—plastic, green, "Your Friendly Railroad," paddle . . . 4.50*

SP—plastic, red, ball top 2.00*

UP—plastic, red, "Golden Spike Centennial," 1869-1969 . . . . 1.50

UP—plastic, red, gold shield logo top 1.50*

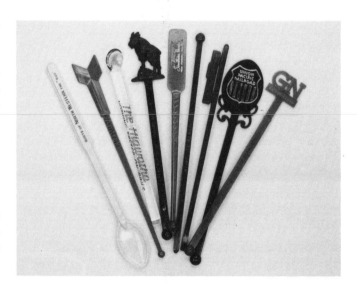

Stir sticks

MISCELLANEOUS

AMTRAK—coaster, plastic backed paper, round with scalloped edges, Amtrak logo at center, blue, red and white . . . . 50¢*

AMTRAK—napkin, paper, logo and slogan, "We've Been Working On The RAILROAD." blue, red and white . . . . . . 50¢

BN—napkin, paper, BN logo, green and white 1.00

CGW—toothpick, 2 quill picks sealed in paper wrapper, marked CGW 2.00

SOO LINE—napkin, paper, white, red logo with red wavy border 2.50

UP—coaster, cardboard, round with scalloped edges, cocktail glass depicted in center, yellow and red 1.00*

UP—coaster, cardboard, round with scalloped edges, winged streamliner motif in center, surrounded by slogan, "Route Of The Daily Domeliners," blue and white 1.00*

UP—toothpick, two sealed in paper wrapper marked with blue Union Pacific shield logo . . . . 25¢*

Coasters and toothpicks

KEYS

Switch keys have always been popular with the railroadiana collector. Thousands of them were made down through the years of bronze or brass, some of steel or iron. The railroad's name or initials were stamped on the front side of the hilt. The letter S (Switch) or other Department letters and a serial number, along with the maker's mark, were generally stamped on the back side. Many collectors suspect that switch keys found without a serial number and maker's hallmark, having only railroad initials stamped on them, are possible fakes. The earlier switch keys, especially from early defunct railroads, with serif letters, tapered barrels with grooved rings around them, nice markings and smooth hand wear, are now realizing fabulous prices.

There were many other railroad marked keys in use for locks on shanties, coal sheds, signal boxes, cabooses, coaches, and so on. These various keys are different in size and shape from the regular switch key and are also being collected. Many recent caboose or coach keys are marked "Adlake" only, and these do not bring the price of those that are railroad marked.

It is recommended that those who are into switch keys subscribe to *Key, Lock & Lantern*, P.O. Box 15, Spencerport, N.Y. 14559 to learn to differentiate between authentic and bogus keys. The buyer should beware when dealing with keys.

SWITCH (Brass unless otherwise noted)

A C L RR—"#19127, Fraim" in banner 22.00

A T & S F RY—"S, 13679 Adlake" 20.00

B & M RR IN NEB—"S,G-401" serifs, tapered barrel w/ring around 135.00

B & O—"C.33498, Fraim," in banner, long barrel 18.00

B & O RR—"S.148314" 15.00

B & O RR CO.—"S, 51566, F-S Hdw. Co.", serifs 25.00

B & M RR—"Bohannan" 22.00

B N INC.—"Adlake," unused 8.50

B R & P R.R.—"S, A & W Co." 30.00

BURLINGTON ROUTE—"S, 8753, A & W Co.," steel key
. . . . .22.00

C C & C RR—"H.C. Jones, Newark, N.J." serifs, tapered barrel w/rings 95.00*

Keys with serif letters and tapered barrels

C.C.C. & I. RY—"J.L. Howard & Co., Hartford, Ct.," serifs, tapered barrel 85.00

C C C & St.L.R.R.—"S, X-8782-B, A & W Co." 20.00

C G W—"Adlake," unused 18.50

C M & P S R.R.—"Loeffelholtz" 50.00

C M & ST P. Ry—"Loeffelholtz" 22.00

C M & St.P.RY—"B," steel key 24.00

C M & ST.P. & P.—"F.-S. Hdwe." 15.00

C N RR—"S, Adlake" 15.00

C N R—"Adlake," unused 13.00

C & NW R.R.—"Bohannan" .30.00

C & NW RY.—"S, A & W Co." 25.00

C & O—"18211, Adlake," unused 14.00

C R I & P RR—"S, 37860, A & W Co." 15.00

C.St.P.M & O RY—"S. Slaymaker" 25.00

C.St. P. M & O RY—"S, A & W Co." 25.00

C & S—"4821, Adlake" 35.00

C V RR—"S, Wilson Bohannan, Brooklyn, N.Y." serifs, tapered barrel 40.00

C & W I RR—"S, A & W Co." 25.00

C & W M RR.—"S A & W Co." 60.00

D & H CO.—"S, 1533," huge letters, serifs 25.00

D & I R RR—"S, K 116," serifs, tapered barrel w/ring around
. . . . 65.00*

D & I R RR—"S, 356," steel, "oiler" key 50.00

D & R G—"S, 475," unused, huge letters 22.00

D L & W—"Fraim" in Keystone 18.00

D M & I R—"4674, Adlake" .25.00

D M & N R—"S, 082, A & W" 75.00

E J & E RY—"S, 8979, Adlake" 25.00

E R R —"S, T. Slaight, Newark, N.J." serifs, tapered barrel
. . . . .55.00

ERIE R R—"F-S Hdwe." 20.00

E L RR—"Adlake," fairly recent 15.00

E St L & S RY—"S, Handlan-Buck, St. Louis, Mo." serifs, tapered barrel 90.00

F & P M R.R.—"J.L. Howard & Co." serifs, tapered barrel
. . . . 65.00

F D D M & S—"Fraim" in Keystone, serifs 42.00

F W & D C—"Adlake" 35.00

FRISCO—"Adlake" 15.00

G & M RR—"S," serifs, tapered barrel 42.00

G B & W RR—"W 110"........................40.00
G N RY—"Fraim" in Keystone..............18.00
G R & I RR—"S," serifs......................65.00
G T W—"Adlake," unused....................16.00
H B L RR—"968, Slaymaker"................15.00
H & ST. JO RR—"S," serifs, tapered barrel w/ring around
....125.00
I C RR—"S, 75793, Adlake"..................15.00
I H B—"Adlake".................................16.00
I H B RR—"Adlake"............................18.00
K C P & G—"W. Bohannan, Newark, N.J." serifs, straight barrel
w/ring...65.00
K C S RY—"10284," huge fancy marking, serifs.....22.00
K & I T—"1634, Adlake"......................25.00
L V R.R.—"S, A & W,"........................20.00
L & N E—"Adlake".............................40.00
L & N RR.—"D, 39976, Dayton" fat short barrel.....20.00
M & I—N P R—"Fraim" in Keystone, double marked..90.00
M & O RR—"Bohannan"........................38.00
M & P DU C RY—"S," serifs, tapered barrel w/ring around
....100.00
M & St.L. RR—"S, W. Bohannan, Brooklyn, N.Y." serifs, tapered
barrel...85.00
M H C & W RR—"S, W. Bohannan, Brooklyn, N.Y." serifs,
tapered barrel................................150.00
M K & T RY—"Fraim" in banner, fat short barrel....25.00
MOPAC RR—"37325, F-S Hdwe."...........15.00
N Y L E & W RR—"S, T. Slaight, Newark, N.J." serifs, tapered
barrel...65.00
N Y C S—"Adlake"............................15.00
N Y O & W RR—"13760, Adlake"...........35.00
N P RR—"S, Slaymaker"......................18.00
N P RY.—"Adlake"............................16.50
OMAHA—"Adlake".............................28.00
O R & N CO—"A & W CO., R & B 586"...........75.00
P R R—"F-S. Hdwe.," knobs around hilt...........25.00

P & L E—"862-B, F. S. Hdwe."..................28.00
P & P U RY.—"466, Adlake"..................36.00
P T R A—"Adlake"..............................18.00
R F & P—"TH, J.H.W. Climax Co., Newark, N.J." serifs45.00
R I & P RY—"S, M. M. Buck & Co., St. Louis, Mo." serifs, tapered
barrel..95.00
RDG CO.—"Adlake"............................20.00
RUTLAND—"Adlake"...........................25.00
St.L & C RR—"S, 268, M.M. Buck & Co., St. Louis, Mo." serifs,
tapered barrel..............................75.00*
St.L & S E RW—"S, M.M. Buck & Co., St. Louis, Mo." serifs,
tapered barrel................................80.00
St. L & S.F. RR.—"S, A & W Co."............35.00
St.L & S W RR.—"Slaymaker"................38.00
St. P M & M RR.—"S"........................100.00
SANTA FE—"S, 29636, A & W Co."..........18.00
SANTA FE ROUTE—"A & W Co., Chicago"........40.00
SOO LINE—"S, A & W Co."....................25.00
S P CO.—"CS-4-S, Adlake"....................15.00
S P CO.—"CS-44, Special 5693"..............18.00
S P CO.—"Freight, A & W Co."................20.00
S P RY.—Huge letters, long barrel............22.50
T & P RY.—"10404, Adlake".................25.00
T P & W—"922, Adlake".......................25.00
T R R A—"9918, Adlake".....................30.00
U P—"28840, Adlake," unused, crude, recent....12.50
U P RR.—"F. S. Hdwe Co."....................15.00
U S T V A—"814, Fraim" in banner.............18.00
V R R—"S, 5884," ornate, big letters.........35.00
WAB. RR—"2104, M.M. Buck & Co., St. Louis, Mo." serifs,
tapered barrel w/ring, steel key............105.00
W C RY.—"Loeffelholtz"......................28.00
W M RY.—"11165, Adlake"...................20.00
W P RR.—"Adlake," unused..................15.00
W & St.P. R.R.—"S, Wilson Bohannan, Brooklyn, N.Y.," serifs,
straight barrel, ring around................135.00

CABOOSE, COACH & MISCELLANEOUS (Brass unless otherwise noted.)

ACL—"Adlake," long solid barrel, caboose..........15.00
B & O RR—"B, No. 107," long hollow barrel, coach..22.00*
BN INC—GN—"Adlake," long solid barrel, caboose...15.00*
C N R—"Mitchell," long hollow barrel, coach........20.00
C N R—"Mitchell," long solid barrel, caboose........15.00*
C M & St.P RR—"STORE DEPT.," short hollow barrel, switch
key type...35.00
C M & St.P RR—"BCC" (baggage car cellar) short hollow barrel,
switch key type..............................38.00
CM St. P & P—"Adlake," long solid barrel, caboose....8.00*
FRISCO—"Yale," flat key, w/Cotton Belt Route tag attached,
general use.....................................35.00*
GN—Short solid barrel, shanty...................12.00*
NP—"Adlake,"long solid barrel, iron key, coach......15.00
NP RY.—"Loeffelholz, U. S. MAIL CAR," small key, double bit,
hollow barrel..................................45.00*

Caboose and coach keys · RR marked

71. Miscellaneous keys - shanties, signal boxes, etc.

M & St. L. RR—"ROAD DEPT.," small switch key type, hollow barrel 45.00*
P R R—"Y65," short hollow barrel, iron key, general use 10.00*
P RR—"Yale," flat key, signal use 10.00
St. L.S.W. RY CO.—short barrel, signal use 15.00*
UP—"Adlake," long solid barrel, caboose 15.00
W RY—"Adlake," long solid barrel, caboose 16.00
Unmarked—"Adlake," long solid barrel, caboose 8.00

Berth and compartment keys

Berth Key—T-shape, 3x4", two-color brass, unmarked 25.00*
Berth & Compartment Key—cross shape, 4x6½", iron w/brass end, unmarked 35.00*

NOTE: The above 2 keys were used by sleeping car porters for unlatching upper berths and to open compartments where pillows, sheets and blankets were stored.

LAMPS

The classification lamps displayed at the front of the steam locomotives, the marker lamps that hung on the rear of the caboose or tail end of the Express trains, the signal lamps used on switch-stands, the interior lamps used in the caboose and coaches, and the track-walker's and inspector's lamps are all being collected today. These bring top prices when found in their all-original condition, bearing a railroad marking. The oil-burning switch-stand lamp appears to be the most popular with the collector.

CLASSIFICATION LAMPS, STEAM LOCOMOTIVE ERA

A pair of these lamps was displayed on the front of the locomotive to indicate its running classification. Each lamp is equipped with a cast iron arm for mounting in the bracket.

"CM&StP RY"—No maker's mark, flat top, electric, two clear lens, inside hand changeable colored glass panes 100.00*
"EJ&E RY - Dressel,"—dome top, oil, two clear lens, inside hand changeable colored glass panes 150.00
"GN RY - Pyle National, 1924,"—diver's helmet type, electric, two clear lens, flip levers to change inner color green lens 125.00
"M SO RR - Adlake,"—dome top, oil, three clear lens, inside hand changeable colored glass panes 175.00

Engine classification and bracket mount

MARKER LAMPS, STEAM ERA

A pair of these was displayed at the tail end of passenger or freight trains to indicate their classification. A cast iron mounting arm is attached at bottom.

"CPR - H.L.Piper,"—dome top, oil, two red, two green bulls-eye
    lens, passenger car 135.00
"C&NW RY - Adlake,"—square top, oil, two red, two green bulls-
    eye lens, caboose 125.00*
"CRI&P RR - Handlan,"—dome top, oil, one red, two green bulls-
    eye lens, passenger car 135.00
"GN RY - Dressel,"—dome top, oil, two red, two green bulls-eye
    lens, passenger car 150.00
"M.ST.P.&S.S.M.RR - Adlake,"—dome top, oil, 3 green, 1 red,
    optical lens, passenger car 200.00
"NP - Adlake,"—square top, oil, one red, three amber bulls-eye
    lens, caboose 125.00

Pair tail-end marker lamps

SWITCH-STAND LAMPS, STEAM ERA

These were mounted on the iron switch-stand post. Each lamp has four lenses, a combination of two red, two green, or two amber. Metal discs or targets of matching colors are sometimes displayed around the lens. The inside oil burning pot is usually missing when found.

"C&NW - Dressel,"—dome top, oil, square post style mount base,
    four prongs 115.00
"CM&StP RY - Star Lantern Co., 1906,"—fluted top, oil, rec-
    tangular post mount base 175.00*

"DM&I R - Adlake,"—square top, oil, bell bottom, fork style mount
    base with four colored metal targets 150.00
"GN RY - Adlake,"—square top, oil, fork style mount base, two
    holes 135.00
"NP - Adlake,"—cannon ball type, "dummy," fork style mount,
    plastic colored reflective lenses 35.00*
"SOO LINE - Armspear,"—dome top, brass, square post style
    mount base, four prongs 165.00*

Switch-stand lamps

Cannon-ball type w/reflective lenses

SEMAPHORE LAMPS, STEAM ERA

These were located behind the metal or wood signal blades at top of the semaphore poles to illuminate the colored lenses.

"GN RR - Adlake,"—oil, fuel pot intact, single clear bulls-eye lens
. . . . 125.00
"NP - Adlake,"—electric, single clear bulls-eye lens. . . . 65.00
"UP - Adlake,"—electric, double clear bulls-eye lens. . . 75.00*

Semaphore lamp

INSPECTOR'S AND TRACK-WALKER'S LAMPS

Inspector's lamps were used by railroad workers to check the journal boxes on rolling stock. The track-walker's lamp is much the same except that it has a red lens at the rear.

"CM&StP RY - Star Lantern Co., Pat. 1910,"—car inspector,
    kerosene. 100.00
"UP RR - C.T. Ham, Pat. 1909,"—track-walker, kerosene, red
    lens at rear. 115.00
"UNMARKED - Dietz,"—no patent date, car inspector, kerosene
    . . . . 50.00
"UNMARKED - Oxweld, 1926,"—car inspector, carbide lamp
    . . . . 75.00
"UNMARKED - Dietz, Pat. 1909,"—track-walker, kerosene, red
    lens at rear. 85.00*

Trackwalker's hand lamp

WALL LAMPS

There were many special design wall lamps for the caboose, bunk cars, passenger cars and shanties. Examples are listed here alphabetically by manufacturer.

ADAMS & WESTLAKE—coach, side wall lamp, round kerosene fount, tall glass chimney, ornate brass bracket arm, 20″ tall, early 250.00

ADAMS & WESTLAKE—bunk car, tin ball-type fuel pot, brass burner, glass chimney, spring holder top. Cast iron wall mount bracket mkd. NP., 16″ tall. 50.00*

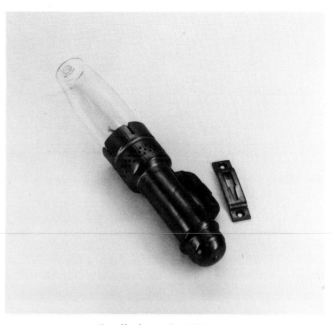

Candle lamp for RPO car

ALADDIN—caboose, brass fuel pot, wall mount arm, glass chimney, mantle and parchment shade, complete . . . 65.00

HANDLAN—shanty, tinware fuel pot, mounting back plate w/smoke deflector, brass burner, glass chimney, mkd. S.P. CO., 16″ tall. 75.00

SAFETY CO. N.Y.—RPO car, brass candle lamp, complete with 5½″tall glass chimney and wall mount bracket. 45.00*

UNMARKED—coach, Pullman berth lamp, wall, electric, 9″ tall, metal, half-round milk white globe with clear opening at side 35.00

UNMARKED—coach, Pullman berth lamp, wall, electric, 9″ tall, brass, white plastic shade. 55.00

Bunk car wall lamp

MISCELLANEOUS LAMP PARTS

LENS—red, 3″ dia., glass, optical, Kopp. 5.00
LENS—red, 5″ dia., glass, ribbed, Corning. 8.00
LENS—green, 5″ dia., glass, optical, Kopp. 9.00*
LENS—amber, 5″ dia., glass, spreadlight, Kopp. 10.00
LENS—blue, 5⅜″ dia., glass, optical, Macbeth. 12.00
LENS—red, 4⅝″ dia., glass, smooth type. 4.00
LENS—green, 5⅜″ dia., plastic, reflector type. 3.50
COUPLING HOOP—for lenses, metal. 2.50*
DAY TARGETS—for switch-stand lamps, metal, enamelled, green, red, yellow 9¾″ dia., each. .5.00*
FOUNT—complete with burner and glass chimney. 22.50*
FORK MOUNT—cast iron, for switch-stand to hold lamp, 6½″ across 15.00

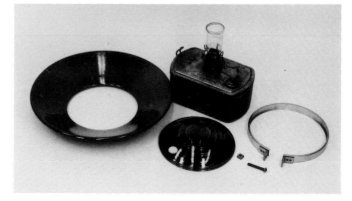

Switch-stand lamp parts

LANTERNS

The earliest lanterns used were the whale-oil type, with no special features. Gradually they were modified to railroad specifications. The railroads identified their lanterns by having their names stamped or embossed somewhere on the frame and also etched or cast on the globe. The manufacturer's name and patent dates are also found on most lanterns. The earlier lanterns came with tall globes; later ones had short globes. An all original lantern with the railroad's name on both frame and globe brings the higher price. A restored lantern with an unmatched or unmarked globe is priced lower. Battery-powered lanterns have replaced these oil-burning lanterns of yesteryear.

Conductor's lanterns are high on the collector's list and usually are sold at auction. They are all brass or nickel plated and generally smaller in size than the switchman's lantern. The globe is clear or sometimes two-color, such as half-green and half-clear. They are not railroad marked unless they were presentation pieces, with the name of the railroad and conductor on the globe or frame. Conductor's lanterns are rare.

Those desiring to know more about lanterns should subscribe to Key Lock & Lantern, P.O. Box 15, Spencerport, N.Y. 14559.

KEY TO ABBREVIATIONS:

P—P after year is the last patent date shown on frame.
NPD—No patent dates on frame.
BB—Bell bottom.
CAST—Raised letters.
TOB—Twist-off bottom.

SWITCHMEN'S HAND LANTERNS

Standard switchmen's lanterns

"A&StL RR"—cast on globe, whale oil type, ca. 1850, rare 750.00
"AT&SF RY"—(lid) "Handlan, 1928-P," red 3¼" globe, etched "AT&SF RY"................................75.00
"AT&SF RY"—(lid) "Adams & Westlake Co. 1933-P," clear 3¼" globe, cast "AT&SF RY".....................95.00
"B&O RR LOCO"—(lid) "Adams & Westlake Co., Adlake Reliable, 1913-P," clear 5⅜" globe cast with capitol dome logo and "LOCO" at rear......................185.00
"B&O RR"—(lid) Keystone, the "Casey," "1903-P," clear 5⅜" globe cast with capitol dome logo...............125.00
"B&A RR"—(lid) "Dietz No. 6," BB, NPD, clear 5⅞" globe cast "B&A RR." Pot slips out from bottom...........200.00

"B&M RR"—(lid) "Adams & Westlake Co., Adlake Reliable, 1913-P," clear 5⅜" globe, cast "B&M RR"........85.00
"BR&P RY"—(lid) "C.T. HAM," BB, "1889-P," clear 5⅜" globe cast "BR&P RY." Pot slips out from bottom......245.00
"BURLINGTON ROUTE"—(lid) "A & W, Adlake Reliable, 1913-P," clear 5⅜" globe cast BURLINGTON ROUTE logo 200.00
"BR"—(lid) "Adlake Kero, 1959-P," clear 3¼" globe, unmarked 40.00
"CNR"—(lid) "Hiram L. Piper, 1955-P," clear 3¼" globe etched "C.N.R" 50.00
"C&O"—(dome) "Adams & Westlake Co. 1945-P," clear 3¼" globe etched "C&O"..........................40.00
"CGW RR"—(lid) "Adams & Westlake Co., Adlake Reliable, 1913-P," red 5⅜" globe cast "CGW RR"........250.00
"C&NW RY"—(dome) "Adams & Westlake Co., Adlake 250 Kero, 1923-P," clear 3¼" globe etched "C&NW"........50.00
"C&NW RY"—(lid) "Adams & Westlake Co., Adlake Reliable, 1913-P," clear 5⅜" globe cast "C&NW RY" in rectangle 135.00
"C&NW RY"—(lid) "Adlake Reliable, 1923-P," clear 5⅜" globe cast THE NORTHWESTERN LINE logo and "CStPM&O RY" below "SAFETY FIRST" at rear................300.00
"CM&StP RY"—(lid) brass top, BB "Adams & Westlake Co.," clear 5⅜" globe cast "CM&StP RY," TOB.......275.00
"CM&StP RY"—(lid) "Armspear, 1913-P" clear 5⅜" globe cast "CM&StP RY"................................85.00
CM&StP RY"—(dome) "Adlake 250 Kero, 1923-P," red 3¼" globe etched "CM&StP"......................60.00

"CMStP&P RR"—(lid) "Adams & Westlake Co., 1934-P," 3¼" green globe etched "CMStP&P RR"............50.00

"CStPM&O RY"—(lid) "Adams & Westlake Co., Adlake Reliable, 1913-P" clear 5⅜" globe cast "CStPM&O" in rectangle 175.00

"CStPM&O RY"—(dome) "Adams & Westlake Co., Adlake Kero, 1923-P," clear 3¼" globe, unmarked............45.00

"CCC&StL RY"—(lid) "Dietz Vesta, 1929-P," clear 4¼" globe cast "CCC&StL RY".....................75.00

"D&H CO"—(lid) "Adams & Westlake Co., Adlake Reliable, 1913-P," clear 5⅜" globe cast the D&H logo.....250.00

"DL&W RR"—(lid) "Dressel, 1913-P," clear 5⅜" globe cast "DL&W RR"..........................150.00

"D&RG RR"—(lid) "Adams & Westlake Co., The Adams, 1909-P," clear 5⅜" globe cast "D&RG RR" large in rectangle 275.00

"D&IR RR"—(lid) "Adams & Westlake Co., Adlake 250 Kero, 1923-P," amber 3¼" globe unmarked...........95.00

"D&IR RR"—(lid) "Adams & Westlake Co., Adlake Reliable, 1913-P," clear 5⅜" globe etched "D&IR RR".....300.00

"DM&N RY"—(lid) "Adams & Westlake Co., 1895-P," clear 5⅜" globe cast 'DM&N RY"..................325.00

"DM&N RY"—(lid) "Adams & Westlake Co., Adlake Reliable," BB, "1912-P," red 5⅜" globe cast "DM&N RY"..375.00

"DW&P"—(lid) "Handlan," NPD, red 4½" Fresnel globe, not railroad marked, large round tin base w/burner.....35.00*

Lanterns with Fresnel globes

"ERIE RR"—(lid) "C.T. HAM, 39 Railroad, 1893-P," clear 5¾" globe cast "E R R CO.," TOB.................135.00

"GN RY"—(lid) "Armspear, 1925-P" clear 3¼" globe cast "G N RY"..95.00

"GN RY"—(lid) "Adams & Westlake Co., Adlake 250 Kero, 1923-P," clear 3¼" globe unmarked............45.00

"GN RY"—(lid) "Adams & Westlake, The Adams, 1909-P," clear 5⅜" globe cast "GN RY. SAFETY ALWAYS" at rear, TOB 195.00

"GN RY"—(lid) "Adams & Westlake Co., Adlake Reliable, 1913-P," amber 5⅜" globe etched "GN RY, SAFETY ALWAYS," at rear.........................250.00

"GN RY"—"Dressel," NPD, blue 3¼" Fresnel globe, not railroad marked 45.00*

"IC RR"—(dome) "Adams & Westlake Co., Adlake 250 Kero, 1923-P," red 3¼" globe etched "IC RR"........65.00

"IC RR"—(lid) "Adams & Westlake Co., The Adams, 1889-P," clear 5⅜" globe cast "IC RR" in rectangle, TOB..150.00

"K&IT RR"—(lid) "Dressel," NPD, red 3¼" globe unmarked 45.00

"LS&MS RY"—(lid) "Adams & Westlake Co., Adlake Reliable, 1913-P," clear 5⅜" globe cast "LS & MS RY," TOB 165.00

"LV RR"—(lid) "RR signal L&L Co., 1889-P," clear 5⅜" globe cast "LV RR," TOB.....................175.00

"MC RR"—(lid) "Armspear, 1889-P," clear 5⅜" globe cast "MC RR," TOB.................................165.00

"M&StL RR"—(dome) "Adams & Westlake Co., Adlake 250 Kero, 1923-P," red 3¼" globe etched "M&StL RR"....110.00

"M&StL RR"—(lid) "Armspear, 1913-P," clear 5⅜" globe cast "M&StL RR".........................325.00

"M&StL RR"—(lid) Keystone, "Casey, 1903-P," red 5⅜" globe cast "M&StL RR".........................350.00

"MOPAC"—(lid) "Handlan," NPD, clear 5⅜" globe cast "M.P.," TOB 150.00

"MOPAC"—(on BB) brass top, "Handlan Buck," NPD, clear 5⅜" globe cast "M.P. SAFETY FIRST" at rear...325.00

"MRR"—(lid) "Dietz Vesta RR Lantern," "BB, 1896-P," clear 5½" globe etched "MRR," TOB...............135.00*

Dietz Vesta lanterns

"NEW YORK CENTRAL"—(lid) "Dietz No. 6," BB, NPD, red 5⅞" globe cast "NEW YORK CENTRAL".......175.00

"NYC RR"—(lid) "Adams & Westlake Co., Adlake Reliable, 1913-P," clear 5⅜" globe cast "NYC RR"........125.00

"NYLE&W RR"—(lid) "Adams & Westlake Co., The Adams, 1889-P," clear 5½" globe cast "NYLE&W RR," TOB 275.00

"NYNH&H RR"—(lid) "Dietz Vesta, 1944-P," clear 4¼" globe cast "NYNH&H RR" 75.00

"NYNH&H RR"—(lid) "Adams & Westlake Co., Adlake Reliable, 1913-P," clear 5⅜" globe cast "NYNH&H RR" . . . 165.00

"NC RY"—(lid) "R.R. Signal L&L Co., 1897-P," clear 5½" globe cast "NCR," TOB 225.00

"NP RY"—(lid) "Adams & Westlake Co., 1938-P," green 3¼" globe etched "NP RY" 65.00

"NP RR"—(lid) "Adams & Westlake Co., The Adams, 1897-P," clear 5⅜" globe cast "NP RR," TOB 200.00

"NP RY"—(lid) "Armspear, 1889-P," clear 5½" globe, cast "NP RY, SAFETY ALWAYS" at rear, TOB 250.00

"PE RY"—(lid) "Adams & Westlake Co., Adlake Reliable, 1913-P," clear 5⅜ globe etched "PE RY, SAFETY FIRST" at rear 135.00

"PRR"—(lid) "Adams & Westlake Co.," BB, "1895-P," clear 5⅜" globe cast "PRR" 195.00

"PRR"—(lid) "Adams & Westlake Co., Adlake Reliable, 1913-P," clear 5⅜" globe cast Keystone logo 125.00

"P&R RY LOCO DEPT"—(lid) "Armspear, 1889-P," clear 5⅜" globe cast "P&R RY," bracket arm, TOB 225.00

"OSL"—(lid) "Adams & Westlake Co., The Adams, 1909-P," clear 5⅜" globe cast "OSL" 300.00

"ROCK ISLAND"—(logo dome) "Adams & Westlake Co., Adlake 250 Kero, 1923-P," clear 3¼" globe unmarked 45.00

"ROCK ISLAND LINES"—(lid) "Adams & Westlake Co., Adlake Reliable, 1913-P," clear 5⅜" globe cast "ROCK ISLAND LINES" 175.00

"SANTA FE A"—(lid) "Adams & Westlake Co., The Adams," BB, "1909-P," clear 5⅜" globe cast "SANTA FE," cross logo 200.00

"SOO LINE"—(lid) "Dressel," NPD, amber 3¼" globe unmarked 65.00

"SOO LINE"—(lid) "Armspear, 1895-P," red 5⅜" globe cast "SOO LINE," TOB 300.00

"SOO LINE"—(lid) "Adams & Westlake Co., Adlake Reliable, 1913-P," clear 5⅜" globe cast "SOO LINE SAFETY ALWAYS" at rear 250.00

"SP CO"—(dome) "Adams & Westlake Co., Adlake 250 Kero, 1923-P," clear 3¼" globe unmarked 40.00

"UNION PACIFIC"—(lid) "Adams & Westlake Co., Adlake Reliable, 1913-P," clear 5⅜" globe, unmarked 65.00

UNMARKED—"Adams & Westlake Co., Adlake Reliable, 1913-P," clear 5⅜" globe unmarked 35.00

UNMARKED—"Adams & Westlake Co., Adlake No. 31," NPD, battery model 15.00

CONDUCTOR'S HAND LANTERNS

Nickel plated conductor's lanterns and the many varieties of early brass types are rare and usually go on the auction block. Examples below are listed alphabetically by manufacturer.

"ADAMS & WESTLAKE CO."—nickel plated, BB, globe half-green, half-clear 500.00*

"ADAMS & WESTLAKE CO."—nickel plated, BB, globe half-green, half-clear, conductor's name etched in wreath 750.00*

"ADAMS & WESTLAKE CO."—nickel plated, BB, "PULLMAN" on base and etched on clear globe 350.00

"M.M. BUCK & CO."—nickel plated, wire ring bottom, clear globe, whale oil burner 375.00

"PETER GRAY, BOSTON"—nickel plated, BB, clear globe 300.00

"F.H. LOVELL & CO."—brass, BB, whale oil burner, early, clear globe 500.00

Conductor's lanterns

SPARE LANTERN GLOBES

"C&O"—etched on 3¼" clear globe 15.00

"C&NW"—etched on 3¼" yellow globe 30.00

"C.St.P.M.&O.RY."—"THE NORTHWESTERN LINE" cast logo front, and cast "SAFETY FIRST" on back of 5⅜" clear globe 200.00

"M&StL RR"—etched on 3¼" red globe 45.00

"MC RR"—cast on 5⅜" clear globe 75.00*

"NEW YORK CENTRAL"—cast on 5¾" bottom lipped clear globe 85.00*

"N.P.R.R."—cast on 5⅜" clear globe, also "SAFETY
ALWAYS,"cast on backside....................65.00
UNMARKED—clear 3¼" globe...................4.00*
UNMARKED—red 3¼" globe...................6.00

TWO COLOR—green over clear conductor's lantern globe
unmarked.................................250.00*
TWO COLOR—green over clear conductor's lantern globe
etched with name..........................350.00*

Spare globes - tall and short styles

Two-color conductor globes

LOCKS

The earlier switch locks were made of brass, later ones of iron or steel. Old brass heart-shaped locks with fancy cast letters on them have gone up in price considerably. Those with authentic factory-stamped markings on the shackle or back panel have also increased in value, especially those from long gone defunct roads. Other letters, numbers, manufacturer's name and patent dates often appear somewhere on the lock. The lock is sometimes found with a short length of iron chain for fastening it to the switch-stand. The railroads had many other types of locks for general purpose use. All of these old railroad marked padlocks are being collected today.

Note of caution: Be aware of spurious locks with stamped markings now coming on the market. A good source for keeping up to date on locks is to become a member of The National Association of Railroadiana Collectors, P.O. Box 15, Spencerport, N.Y., 14559.

SWITCH (all are brass unless otherwise noted)

"AT&SF RY"—stamped on shackle, heart shape, "UNION
BRASS," ca. 1880s (scarce)...................175.00
"BCR&M RR"—incised on shackle, heart shape, "ADRIAN
MICH," ca. 1870s (rare).....................300.00
"BURLINGTON"—stamped on shackle, steel, brass rivets, no
maker's mark.................................15.00
"CM&StP RR"—cast on back panel, heart shape,
"LOEFFELHOLZ"................................95.00
"CM&StP RR"—stamped on back, "ADLAKE" on drop, steel,
iron chain, 1923.............................20.00
"CMStP&P RR"—stamped on shackle, steel, "Pat. March 5, 1929,
FRAIM," chain...............................25.00
"CMStP&P RR"—stamped on shackle, heart shape, "HANSL
MFG", 1956, chain...........................35.00
"C&NW"—stamped on shackle, heart shape, "SLAYMAKER"
chain, early 1900s...........................75.00
"CPR"—raised on key drop, steel, "MITCHELL".....22.00*
"CRI&P RR"—stamped on shackle, heart shape, "UNION BRASS
CO.," ca. 1880s (scarce).....................175.00

Standard steel clad switch locks

"CRI&P"—stamped on back, "Pat. Mar 20, 1920", steel, "ADLAKE" on drop.........................20.00*

"CStPM&O RY"—stamped on shackle, "Pat. Sept. 24, 1912," steel, "ADLAKE" on drop, chain...............30.00

"CStPM&O RY"—stamped on shackle, heart shape, "SLAYMAKER", chain, early 1900s............125.00

"DL&W"—stamped on shackle, heart shape, "FRAIM", chain, early 1900s................................85.00

"D&SF"—stamped on shackle, heart shape, "EAGLE LOCK CO." (rare).......................................200.00

"FE&MV"—stamped on shackle, heart shape, "Pat. 1879, BOHANNAN"..............................195.00

"GN RY"—stamped on shackle, steel, "SLAYMAKER, Pat. 1915"
....25.00

"GN RY"—cast ornate into entire back side, heart shape, "SLAYMAKER," early 1900s.................250.00

"MRR CO"—cast on back panel, heart shape, "MILLER LOCK CO.," early 1900s.........................150.00

"MHC&W RR"—incised on shackle, heart shape, "Pat. June 25, '79, W. BOHANNAN," chain (rare)............300.00

"MK&T"—stamped on shackle, steel, "SLAYMAKER" on drop, 1948, chain....................................15.00

"M&StL RY"—stamped on shackle, steel, "F.S.HDW." on drop, 1938, chain.................................35.00*

"NYB&M RR"—stamped on back panel, heart shape, "T. SLATCH," ca. 1870s.........................175.00

"NPR"—cast on back panel, heart shape, "FRAIM," 1911
....100.00

"NORTHERN PACIFIC"—cast on back panel, "SWITCH" raised, heart shape, "ADLAKE" on drop...............95.00

"N&W RY"—cast on entire back side, heart shape, 1952, no maker's mark.................................95.00

"PRR CO"—cast ornately on entire back, heart shape, "FRAIM," 1911.......................................110.00

"StPM&M RR"—stamped on shackle, heart shape, "UNION BRASS CO.," 1880s (rare)....................200.00*

"StPM&M"—cast on back panel, "DAYTON MFG CO." (rare)
....250.00*

Brass heart-shape with cast and stamped letters

"StP&P RR"— stamped on shackle, heart shape, "UNION BRASS CO." 1870s, (rare)........................300.00

"StPSY CO"—stamped on shackle, heart shape, "A&W CO." on drop 55.00

"SOO LINE"—stamped on shackle, steel, "ADLAKE" embossed on drop, no maker's mark, recent...............10.00

"SO. RY."—stamped on shackle, banjo style with brass rivets, "YALE," chain...............................35.00

"UP RR"—cast on back with "SWITCH", heart shape, 1951, chain, no maker's mark.......................75.00

"UNION PACIFIC"—cast on back panel, "SWITCH CS-1" raised, heart shape, "ADLAKE," chain..................50.00

"UNION PACIFIC"—cast on back panel, "CLOSE THE LOCK TO GET THE KEY OUT" cast on drop, "A&W CO" on shackle, chain..............................65.00

SIGNAL (all are brass unless otherwise noted)

"AT&SF RY"—stamped on bottom edge, "EAGLE LOCK CO.", ca. 1930s....................................35.00

"B&M RR"—stamped on shackle, small heart shape, "WILSON BOHANNAN".................................25.00

"B&O"—cast in front circle, "SIGNAL DEPT." incised, "YALE"
....18.00*

"C&A"—stamped on shackle with "SIGNAL," small heart shape, "MILLER" on drop.........................20.00

"D&H"—stamped "THE D&H" on front, "SIGNAL" at bottom edge, "YALE".....................................22.00

"DL&W RR"—cast on back panel, "REMOVE KEY WHEN LOCKING" cast on key drop, "SLAYMAKER".....25.00

"GN RY"—raised on back panel, "REMOVE KEY WHEN LOCKING" cast on key drop, "SLAYMAKER".........28.00*

"IC RR"—raised on back panel, small, heart shape, no maker's mark.....................................15.00

"JERSEY CENTRAL LINES"—stamped in circle on front, signal number on back, no maker's mark.............16.00

"NICKEL PLATE RR"—cast in front circle, "SIGNAL DEPT." incised, "YALE"............................22.00

"P&LE RR"—cast in front circle, "SIGNAL DEPT." incised, "YALE" 26.00

Brass signal locks

"ROCK ISLAND LINES"—stamped on front with "SIGNAL" below. "CORBIN" with patent numbers on back.... 18.00

"SOO LINE"—stamped on shackle, with "SIGNAL, REMOVE KEY WHEN LOCKING" cast on drop, small heart shape, 1930s, no maker's mark...................... 38.00

"SOUTHERN RY"—cast on back panel with "SIGNAL," large heart shape, "A&W CO." on key drop........... 55.00

"UP RR"—stamped on front, with "CS-61 SIGNAL USE NO OIL," small, chain, no maker's mark................. 18.00*

"WABASH"—Flag emblem cast in circle, "SIGNAL DEPT." incised, "YALE"............................... 30.00

"M&StL RR"—stamped on shackle, steel, heart shape, "F-S HDW CO.," shanty................................... 45.00*

"MStP&SSM"—stamped on shackle, brass, heart shape, "SHOREHAM SHOPS" on drop, "F-S HDW. 1932" on back side..................................... 125.00

"RY. EX. AGY."—stamped on shackle and back side, steel, "Pat. 11-21-05," general use, no maker's mark.......... 35.00

"SOUTHERN PACIFIC"—Sunset logo cast on front, brass, heart shape, early 1900s, general use, no maker's mark.. 85.00

"UNION PACIFIC"—with "CS-21 ROADWAY & BRIDGE DEPARTMENT" cast on entire back, brass, heart shape, "ADLAKE" chain............................. 45.00

MISCELLANEOUS

"B&O RR"—stamped on front, small steel, brass rivets, shanty, no maker..................................... 15.00*

"CB&Q RR"—stamped on back, steel, brass rivets, "CORBIN," general use................................... 22.00

"CB&Q RR"—raised on drop, small steel, shanty, no maker's mark..................................... 14.00*

"CStPM&DM"—stamped on shackle, steel, shield shape, "MILLER" embossed on key drop, shanty........ 25.00*

"FRISCO"—cast on front, "DON'T USE OIL BUT PLENTY OF GRAPHITE" on back, brass, "KEEN KUTTER," general use 175.00

"GN RY"—stamped on shackle, steel, shield shape, "MILLER LOCK CO.," 1920s, general use................. 25.00

"M&StL RR"—stamped on front shackle, "ROAD DEPT." on rear shackle, brass, small heart shape, "FRAIM"... 75.00

Miscellaneous general use locks

LOCOMOTIVE BUILDER'S PLATES

Locomotives have always been identified with the name of their builders by means of a metal plaque usually affixed on each side of the smokebox. They were made in various shapes and sizes, with the name of the locomotive company, serial number, location of the works, and year date of completion. Builder's plates from the steam era are much in demand and have become scarce and valuable. Examples of plates from the more common producers are listed here. Reproductions have come on the market, so be wary.

AMERICAN—"American Locomotive Company," Serial No., "Schenectady Works, July, 1912," brass rectangle with rounded corners, 7½" x 14"......................... 150.00*

BALDWIN—"Built By The Baldwin Locomotive Works, Philadelphia, Pa.," Serial No., "August, 1913," bronze rectangle, 3½" x 9"........................... 125.00*

BALDWIN—"The Baldwin Locomotive Works," Serial No., "Philadelphia, U.S.A., August, 1914," bronze disc, 9¼" diameter.................................. 200.00*

BALDWIN—"Baldwin Locomotive Works, Philadelphia, U.S.A., Burnham Williams & Co.," Serial No., "August, 1905," brass disc, 16½"diameter........................ 300.00

LIMA—"Lima Locomotive Works, Incorporated, December, 1939," brass, diamond shape, 9¼" x 16"........ 275.00

Cast bronze steam locomotive plates

PORTER—"H.K. Porter Company, Pittsburgh, U.S.A.," Serial No., cast brass, shield shape, 8⅞" x 8¼" 250.00
ALCO-GE—diesel locomotive cast iron rectangle plate, "American Locomotive Co., Schenectady, N.Y.," Serial No., "November, 1948," Alco and GE logos, rectangle plate, 6¼" x 12¼" 95.00
GM-EMD—diesel locomotive stainless steel rectangle plate, Class 0-4-4-0, Serial No., date 1-16-42, silver letters on black, 4¾" x 14¾" 50.00*
GM-EMD—diesel locomotive stainless steel oval plate, Class 0-4-4-0, Serial No., date Mar. 54, original red and blue colors on silver, 4⅛" x 15" 30.00

Stainless steel diesel locomotive plate

LUGGAGE STICKERS

During the Golden Years of the passenger train when travel by train was the way to go, colorful paper labels with a gummed back were handed out at ticket counters to be pasted on suitcases and valises. It was a common sight to see these stickers on luggage everywhere, toted by tourists, advertising that they were riding the popular "name trains" and had been or were going to the many vacation spots throughout the country. These unused luggage stickers are now being sought after. Those from the steam era are harder to find and worth more than those issued during the waning years of rail travel.

"BURLINGTON ROUTE"—Cut-out profile of Buffalo Bill with slogan, "Yellowstone Park via Cody Road" 15.00
"BURLINGTON ROUTE"—Round sticker, aluminum foil type in blue, depicting the silver ZEPHYR at center 8.00*

Luggage with glued-on stickers

"C&O"—Round sticker showing sleepy kitten within a heart entitled "THE GEORGE WASHINGTON," "Sleep like a Kitten" 6.00
"C&NW"—Small square sticker with slogan, "The Famous 400" "6½ hrs. Chicago-Twin Cities, 409 miles-390 minutes" 5.00
"CHICAGO & NORTHWESTERN-UNION PACIFIC"—Hexagon style sticker showing yellow streamliner, CITY OF DENVER and slogan, "World's Fastest Long Distance Train". 10.00

"GN RY"—Large round sticker, mountain goat atop logo encircled with slogan, "See American First, Glacier National Park" 20.00
"GN RY"—Large round sticker, white goat atop mountain in red center, with "Great Northern Railway" in blue on white 4.00*
"MILWAUKEE ROAD"—Round sticker depicting "HIAWATHA" steam train No. 1 at center, with slogan "Nothing Faster On Rails" below 7.50
"MILWAUKEE ROAD"—Round sticker depicting the electric train, "OLYMPIAN" in black, purple and orange colors 8.00
"MO-PAC"—Cut-out sticker of black steam engine with red buzz-saw logo entitled "THE SUNSHINE SPECIAL" with ad copy below 15.00
"MO-PAC"—Cut-out sticker of black steam engine and red buzz-saw logo entitled "THE SCENIC LIMITED" with ad copy below 15.00
"MO-PAC"—Large red and white buzz-saw logo 3.50
"NORTHWESTERN-UNION PACIFIC"—Round label type sticker with wavy border entitled "The Streamliner CITY OF DENVER" 3.00
"NORTHWESTERN-UNION PACIFIC"—Round label type sticker with wavy border entitled "The Streamliner CITY OF LOS ANGELES" 3.00
"PRR"—Burgundy red keystone logo entitled "Travel By Train" 3.50
"SANTA FE"—Square type, blue and silver, with Indian and logo at center, entitled "SUPER CHIEF" 3.50*
"SANTA FE"—Round sticker, red logo on yellow at upper right, entitled "EL CAPITAN" 2.50*
"SP"—Round logo, "SOUTHERN PACIFIC LINES" in blue, white and gold 3.50

MAGAZINES

Literally thousands of railroad magazines were published down through the years for both the trainman and the general public. Many were put out by the Brotherhood for the engineer, fireman, carman and other members. Also, the railroad companies published various inter-company magazines for their employees. Railroad magazines for the public, both pulp and slick paper, have been in publication from the turn of the century up to the present time.

A series of dime novels, published weekly for the American youth, was issued around the turn of the century, with names such as *PLUCK AND LUCK, WORK AND WIN,* and *BRAVE AND BOLD,* to name a few. These early pulps had eye-catching front covers with illustrations of exciting railroad scenes, and are being picked up, too. Copies of all these various magazines in fine condition are bringing good prices today.

BROTHERHOOD

FREIGHT HANDLERS AND RAILWAY CLERKS JOURNAL—
Sept. 1912...............................6.00*
LOCOMOTIVE ENGINEER'S JOURNAL—September, 1920
................................3.50*
LOCOMOTIVE ENGINEER'S JOURNAL—March, 1940.2.00
LOCOMOTIVE FIREMAN'S MAGAZINE—June, 1905...5.00
LOCOMOTIVE FIREMEN AND ENGINEMEN'S MAGAZINE—
October, 1911..............................4.00
RAILWAY AGE AND SERVICE MAGAZINE—March, 1882
....10.00
RAILWAY CARMEN'S JOURNAL—May, 1908.........5.00*
RAILROAD TRAINMEN'S JOURNAL—February, 1894..8.00
RAILROAD TRAINMEN'S JOURNAL—May, 1903.....5.00
THE RAILROAD TRAINMAN—January, 1940.........2.00

Brotherhood magazines

INTER-COMPANY

MAINE-CENTRAL RAILROAD EMPLOYEES MAGAZINE, Vol.
3, No.'s 1-12, Oct. 1946-Sept. 1947, complete set..10.00*
NORTHWESTERN RAILWAY MAGAZINE—C&NW RR, Oc-
tober, 1923...................................4.00
ROCK ISLAND MAGAZINE—CRI&P RR, October, 1922, 70th
Anniversary number..........................15.00
THE FOUR TRACK NEWS—NYC&H RR, April, 1903.5.00
THE MILWAUKEE ROAD MAGAZINE—CMStP&P RR,
July/Aug., 1957..............................1.50

Inter-company issues

PUBLIC

MODERN RAILROAD—March, 1955...............1.50
RAILROAD MAGAZINE—(pulp), May, 1942..........3.00
RAILROAD MAGAZINE—(pulp) Complete set, Jan-Dec. 1938
....36.00
RAILROADMAN'S MAGAZINE—(pulp) March, 1939....3.00

RAILROAD STORIES—(pulp) May, 1932.............3.50
RAILROAD STORIES—12 copies, complete, 1934....42.00
RAILWAY PROGRESS—Complete set, January-December, 1954
....8.00
TRAINS MAGAZINE—(small) February, 1944.........2.00

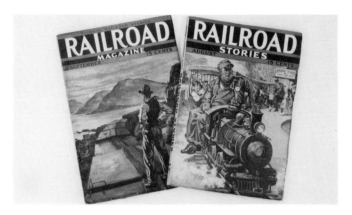

Pulp periodicals

TRAINS MAGAZINE—(large) January, 1952..........1.50
TRAINS MAGAZINE—Complete set, bound, Vol. I, Nov.
1940-July 1941................................50.00
TRAINS MAGAZINE—Complete set, bound, Vol. 27, Nov.
1966-Oct. 1967.............................30.00

BOY'S WEEKLYS

BUFFALO BILL WEEKLY— "Buffalo Bill At Canon Diablo,"
May 26, 1917................................7.50*
FAME AND FORTUNE WEEKLY—"Striking His Gait," or "The
Perils of a Boy Engineer," September 1, 1916......9.50*
THE GEM LIBRARY—"Dick, The Boy Engineer," or "On The
Right Track," April 1, 1896....................15.00*
PLUCK AND LUCK—"Dick, The Apprentice Boy," or "Bound
To Be An Engineer," March 7, 1906.............10.00*
TIP TOP WEEKLY—"Frank Merriwell's Advancement," or
"Engineer Of The Mountain Express," August 27, 1898
....12.50
WORK AND WIN—"Fred Fearnot's New Trouble," or "Up
Against A Monopoly," December 19, 1902........11.50*

Boy's Weekly's

MAPS

Roll-down maps issued by the railroads were used in classrooms and libraries. Large system maps hung on the walls of railroad ticket offices and depots. Tourist guide maps were handed out freely by the railroads. Private firms also published railroad maps for the public's use. There are also railroad commissioner's state maps and a wide array of other old railroad maps issued down through the years. The early rare maps bring the higher prices.

C&NW—Lakes and resorts in Central Wisconsin, 20″ x 22″, 1904
....20.00
CRAM'S—Railroad pocket map, Wisconsin, unfolds 19″ x 24″,
soft cover, 1885...............................25.00*
GOLDTHWAIT'S—Railroad map, New England States, Canada,
Eastern New York, unfolds 18″ x 24″, hard cover, 1850, (rare)
....50.00*
GN RY—Topographic map of Glacier National Park, Montana,
unfolds 31″ x 34″, cloth backed, hard cover, 1922.20.00
M&S RR—Framed wall map, 23″ x 39″, lines and connections,
1856 (rare)...................................75.00

NP—Mounted wall map, 23″ x 35″, line and connections, 1893
....35.00
ROCK ISLAND—Travel folder map, 18″ x 32″, U.S. and System,
1924..7.50*
SP—U.S. map, 41″ x 51″, wall, roller type, 1951.....25.00*
StPM&M RR—Sectional, 24″ x 34″, Lands For Sale, 1916
....35.00
UP—Tourist folding map, 18″ x 32″, U.S. and System, 1922
....8.50*
R.R. COMMISSIONER—Map of Minnesota, 31″ x 50″, folding
pocket type, 1925.............................6.00*

R.R. COMMISSIONER—Map of Montana, unfolds 40″ x 53″, cloth backed, hard cover, 1908.................25.00*

Miscellaneous railroad maps

Wall map

MEDALLIONS, MEDALS AND TOKENS

Railroads issued medallions, medals and tokens down through the years to commemorate special events in their history, their anniversaries, advertising and World Fair souvenirs. Most were made of bronze or brass, in various diameters, occasionally rectangular in shape, depicting locomotives and historical events. Special medallions were also issued to railroads for their safety efforts and prevention of accidents. Prices are based on the scarcity of the medallion, medal or token.

B&O—1827-1927 100th Anniversary medallion, bronze, 2¾″ diameter, Tom Thumb and modern passenger train, obverse and reverse....................................85.00

BCR&N—Advertising medallion, pewter, 2¾″ diameter, "Albert Lea Route, The Burlington, Cedar Rapids & Northern Ry." within wreath on obverse, list of cities served on reverse, ca. 1890s....................................95.00

C&NW—Safety Award medallion, bronze, 2¾″ diameter, E.H. Harriman profile on obverse, trainman walking track on reverse 50.00

CM&StP—Medallion, bronze, 3″ diameter, w/rimmed ½″ edge, logo with "To Puget Sound Electrified" on obverse, "Special Apprentices Staff Meeting, Milwaukee, 1925" on reverse 85.00

D&H—1827-1927 100th Anniversary medallion, bronze, rectangular, 2½″ x 4″ commemorating the Stourbridge Lion's first successful trip, August 8, 1829, at Honesdale, Pa. 100.00

GN RY—Memorial medallion, 1916, bronze, 3″ diameter, James J. Hill profile obverse, wreath and year dates reverse 25.00

IC—1851-1951 100 year Centennial medallion, bronze, 3″ diameter, diamond logo and map, obverse and reverse 38.00*

IC—1851-1951 100 year Centennial medal, bronze, smaller size, 1⅜″ diameter, identical to the larger issue........22.50

Centennial and advertising medallions

ROCK ISLAND—Anniversary medal, bronze, 1¼″ diameter, logo and "70th Anniversary, 1852-1922" obverse, Lincoln profile, trains, bridge and history on reverse............35.00*

SANTA FE—1868-1968-2068, Second Century Progress medal, brass, 1½″ diameter, logo and progress, obverse and reverse 10.00

StLSW—Advertising medallion, bronze, 3″ diameter, "St. Louis Southwestern Railway Lines" around edge w/floral spray, "Cotton Belt Route" logo, diesel freight, lightning bolt and words "Blue Streak Fast Freight" on obverse, reverse blank, ca. 1950s 65.00*

Anniversary medal - obverse and reverse

Aluminum token - 1934 lucky piece

UP—1869-1969 Centennial Celebration medallion, bronze, 2½" diameter, Golden Spike obverse, two locomotives reverse 20.00
UP—1869-1969 Centennial Celebration medal, bronze, smaller size, 1¼", identical to the larger issue 10.00

UNION PACIFIC—Token, aluminum, 1¼" diameter, streamline diesel, "1934 Lucky Piece" on obverse, history data reverse 5.00*
UNION PACIFIC—Token, aluminum, 1¼" diameter, 1939, "Golden Gate International Exposition, San Francisco Bay" on obverse, logo and streamliners on reverse 5.00
UNION PACIFIC—Token, aluminum, 1¼" diameter, "1940 Lucky Piece," logo and trains on both sides 5.00

PASSES

Passes were issued by the railroads down through the years to officials of railroads, newspapermen, politicans, clergymen, and other favored persons. Passes from the 1850s and 1860s bring top prices. Passes with locomotives, trains, picturesque scenes and ornate designs on them are highly desirable and priced according to their pictorial or historical significance, as are those from obscure, short lived and now defunct roads. Passes from the 1940s up to the present time have lower value.

Railroads also issued passes to their employees and their families. These were either annual passes or were good for one trip only. They were usually made of card stock, but a great many were made of paper stock, larger than the standard size pass. Employee passes are generally priced lower, exceptions being the uncommon and long gone railroads.

There were also passes issued by express companies, telegraph companies, omnibus lines, the Pullman Company, etc., in connection with the railroads allowing the holder to occupy a Pullman seat or berth, transport packages, send telegrams, cross a river on a toll bridge or ferryboat, get transportation between depots and hotels, and so on, without charge. Value on these various railroad-related passes are based according to their rarity.

PUBLIC

"ALABAMA CENTRAL RAILROAD"—1876 . . . . 15.00
"ALLEGHENY VALLEY RAILROAD"—1873, locomotive 20.00
"ATLANTIC, MISSISSIPPI & OHIO R.R."—1873, ornate engravings 30.00
"ATLANTIC & PACIFIC R.R."—1873, Eads bridge, St. Louis 30.00
"AVON, GENESEO & MT. MORRIS RR."—1868 . . . . . 20.00
"BALTIMORE & OHIO R.R."—1873, train 20.00
"BUFFALO, ROCHESTER & PITTSBURGH"—1894 . . . 8.00
"BURLINGTON & LAMOILLE RR."—1884 . . . . 10.00

"BURLINGTON, CEDAR RAPIDS & NORTHERN RY."—1900 . . . . 12.00
"CHESAPEAKE & OHIO R.R."—1930 . . . . 3.00
"CHESHIRE & ASHEULUT RR."—1873 . . . . : . 10.00
"CHICAGO & ALTON R.R."—1865, eagles and flags . . 35.00
"CHICAGO & ALTON R.R."—1895, full length passenger train 25.00
"CHICAGO & ALTON R.R."—1896, Father Time in locomotive cab, colored lithograph 25.00
"CHICAGO GREAT WESTERN RY."—1898, colorful maple leaf emblem 15.00

"CHICAGO, MILWAUKEE & ST. PAUL RY."—1875..15.00
"CHICAGO & NORTHWESTERN RY."—1897........8.50
"CHICAGO & ROCK ISLAND R.R."—1865, train on bridge and steamboat.....................................35.00
"CHICAGO, ST. PAUL & KANSAS CITY RY."—1891, clergyman's ½ fare permit.....................10.00
"CHICAGO, ST. PAUL, MPLS. & OMAHA RY."—1912.8.00
"CHICAGO, SOUTH SHORE & SOUTH BEND"—1963-1964
....2.00
"CORNING, COWANESQUE & ANTRIM RY."—1876, picturesque.....................................20.00
"DAYTON & UNION R.R."—1868, ornate...........25.00
"DELAWARE, LACKAWANNA & WESTERN RR."—1869
....10.00
"DULUTH SOUTH SHORE & ATLANTIC RY."—1891, picturesque harbor scene........................15.00
"ELGIN, JOLIET & EASTERN RY."—1895..........8.00
"ERIE RAILWAY"—1874, picturesque.............18.00
"EVANSVILLE & TERRE HAUTE R.R."—1897.......6.00
"FLINT & PERE MARQUETTE RY."—1873, train on covered bridge......................................20.00
"FLORIDA CENTRAL & PENINSULAR R.R."—1896..8.00
"FLORIDA EAST COAST RY."—1899..............6.00
"GEORGIA, SOUTHERN & FLORIDA RY."—1899....6.00
"GREAT NORTHERN RY."—1911..................6.00
"GREAT WESTERN RY. OF CANADA"—1865, train on suspension bridge.................................30.00
"GULF & SHIP ISLAND R.R."—1898..............7.00
"ILLINOIS CENTRAL R.R."—1865, picturesque depot scene
....30.00
"INDIANA, DECATUR & WESTERN RY."—1896.....7.00
"INTERNATIONAL & GREAT NORTHERN RR."—1899, American & Mexican flags.....................10.00
"IOWA CENTRAL RY."—1898, farming & industry scene
....12.00
"JACKSONVILLE, LOUISVILLE & ST. LOUIS"—1895.6.00
"KANSAS PACIFIC RY."—1873..................10.00
"KANSAS CITY SOUTHERN"—1909................5.00
"LACROSSE & MILWAUKEE R.R."—1863.........20.00
"LAKE ERIE & WESTERN RY."—1882, editor's pass, photo of bearer (rare).............................50.00*

"LAKE SHORE & MICHIGAN SOUTHERN RY."—1895
....7.00
"LOUISVILLE, CINCINNATI & LEXINGTON R.R." Shortline—1873, train on bridge.................20.00
"MANISTEE & NORTHWESTERN R.R."—1896, train and lake steamer......................................25.00
"MANITOBA & NORTHWESTERN RY. OF CANADA"—1895, locomotive.....................................12.00
"MICHIGAN CENTRAL R.R."—1865, Great Central Union depot
....35.00
"MPLS. & ST. LOUIS RY."—1944-45............4.00
"MPLS. ST. PAUL & SAULT STE. MARIE RY."—1917
....6.00
"MINNESOTA & NORTHWESTERN RR."—1887.....20.00*

Plain style cardstock pass

"MISSOURI PACIFIC R.R."—1920................4.00
"MOBILE & BIRMINGHAM R.R."—1897, passenger train
....15.00
"NEW YORK CENTRAL"—1953-1954.............3.00
"NEW YORK, PENNSYLVANIA & OHIO R.R."—1883, clergyman's certificate.......................12.00
"NORTH MISSOURI R.R."—1865, 4-4-0 locomotive...45.00*

Early pass picturing locomotive

"NORTHERN PACIFIC R.R."—1880..............20.00
"OGDENSBURG & LAKE CHAMPLAIN R.R."—1870.12.00
"OHIO RIVER R.R."—1895, locomotive..........15.00
"OIL CREEK & ALLEGHENY RIVER RY."—1873, oil well derrick......................................16.50
"PENNSYLVANIA RAILROAD"—1868, editorial.....20.00
"PERE MARQUETTE R.R."—1902................6.00

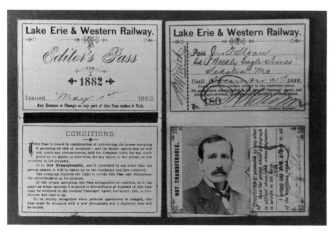

Pass with photo of bearer

"PITTSBURGH & CONNELSVILLE R.R."—1870.....18.00
"PLANT SYSTEM RYS."—1897..................15.00
"QUEEN & CRESCENT ROUTE"—1895...........6.50
"QUINCY, ALTON & ST. LOUIS R.R."—1873......10.00
"ROCK ISLAND & PEORIA RY."—1895, train......15.00
"ROME, WATERTOWN & OGDENSBURGH R.R."—1868
....15.00
"ST. LOUIS & IRON MOUNTAIN R.R."—1865, primitive train
....25.00
"ST. LOUIS & SAN FRANCISCO RY."—1881, locomotive
    engraving..................................20.00
"ST. PAUL & DULUTH R.R."—1892, engraved scenes20.00
"ST. PAUL, MPLS, & MANITOBA RY."—1881, Jas. J. Hill
    signature..................................50.00

"ST. PAUL & PACIFIC R.R."—1877..............15.00
"SOUTHERN MINNESOTA R.R."—1879...........15.00
"SOUTHERN PACIFIC"—1946-1948..............3.00
"TALLASEE & MONTGOMERY RY."—1896........6.00
"TAURES & GULF R.R."—1895, train...........15.00
"TOLEDO, PEORIA & WARSAW RY."—1869......15.00
"UTAH CENTRAL R.R."—1876.................15.00
"VERMONT CENTRAL & VT. CANADA R. ROADS"—1870,
    depot scene.............................18.00
"WABASH, ST. LOUIS & PACIFIC RY."—1896......12.00
"WESTERN UNION R.R."—1869.................10.00
"WISCONSIN CENTRAL LINES"—1889, train on bridge
....15.00
"YAZOO & MISSISSIPPI VALLEY R.R."—1898......7.50

EMPLOYEE

"CHICAGO, MILWAUKEE & ST. PAUL RY."—1887, annual
....9.50
"CHICAGO & NORTHWESTERN RY."—1884, trip...10.00
"COLORADO MIDLAND"—1916, annual...........22.50
"DULUTH & IRON RANGE R.R."—1892, trip.......9.00
"GREAT NORTHERN RY."—1901, time............6.50
"GREEN BAY, WINONA & ST. PAUL R.R."—1889, trip
....9.50
"HOCKING VALLEY RY."—1908, time............5.50
"ILLINOIS CENTRAL R.R."—1892, trip...........8.50
"MICHIGAN CENTRAL R.R."—1894, trip..........8.00
"MPLS. & ST. LOUIS R.R."—1930, annual.........4.00
"MISSOURI PACIFIC RY."—1899, trip.............7.50*
"NORTHERN PACIFIC R.R."—1904, exchange trip....6.00
"PHILADELPHIA, WILMINGTON & BALTIMORE
    R.R."—1899, annual.........................7.50
"SOUTHERN RAILWAY"—1914, annual...........4.00

Employee trip pass

"WISCONSIN CENTRAL LINES"—1892, trip........10.00

MISCELLANEOUS

"ADAMS EXPRESS COMPANY"—1895...........10.00
"ILLINOIS & ST. LOUIS BRIDGE"—1876, bridge and river scene
....25.00
"NATIONAL EXPRESS COMPANY"—1902.........8.00
"NATIONAL MAIL COMPANY"—1895, stagecoach...25.00
"PARMELEE CO. CHICAGO OMNIBUS LINE"—1903..8.00*
"POSTAL TELEGRAPH-CABLE COMPANY"—1902...8.00
"PULLMAN'S PALACE CAR COMPANY"—1873, Geo. M.
    Pullman signature.........................45.00*
"SENECA LAKE STEAM NAVIGATION CO."—1895, steamboat
    and train...............................25.00
"UNITED STATES EXPRESS COMPANY"—1899, horseshoe
    trademark.................................10.00*
"WESTERN EXPRESS COMPANY"—1900..........7.50
"WESTERN UNION TELEGRAPH COMPANY"—1873
....16.00*
"WIGGINS FERRY COMPANY"—1876.............18.00

"WOODRUFF SLEEPING & PARLOR COACH CO."—1873,
    Jonah Woodruff signature..................30.00

Express, Western Union, Pullman, Omnibus

PINBACKS

Thousands of pinbacks were worn by railroad employees and also handed out freely by the railroads to the general public. They carried safety slogans, promotional advertising, named passenger trains, etc.. Some have a history dating back to the turn of the century. There are many collectors for these colorful old celluloid buttons, and they are getting scarce, with prices on the increase.

Railroad-related pinbacks are also included in this category, and some of these are listed at the end.

AMTRAK—"Tracks Are Back!" black letters on white, 2⅛″ diameter 4.00

AMTRAK—1973, "Ride The Turbo!" white on aqua, 1¾″ diameter 3.00

ACL—"100% Safety, 1931" white on purple, ⅞″ diameter 6.00

BCR&N RY—Red diamond logo on white, ⅞″ diameter (rare) 25.00

BN—1967, "Safety-Courtesy-Dependability," white goat on blue, 1¼″ diameter 5.00

BN—1969, "Pace Your Life To Live," white goat on gold, 1¼″ diameter 5.00

BURLINGTON ROUTE—Logo, tracks, 1850-1940, white background, 11⁄16″ diameter 4.00

BURLINGTON ROUTE—Silver Zephyr on dark blue, 1″ diameter 5.00

CPR—Beaver atop red shield logo, "Get Your Canadian Home From The Canadian Pacific," black on white, 1″ diameter 20.00

C&O RY—Chessie kitten on white background, 1½″ diameter 15.00

CC&L—"The Straight Line," black and red on white, ¾″ diameter 5.00

CM&StP RY—Red logo, "Safety First" on white, 1″ diameter 6.00

CM&StP RY—"Opportunity, Orchard Homes, Government Homesteads," red logo on white and yellow, 1½″ diameter 20.00

C&NW LINE—Black and red logo, and "Passenger Agent" on white, 2¼″ diameter 8.00

GN RY—Logo at center w/shock of wheat, "Montana For Me, 320 Acres, Free Farms" around edge. Black/yellow/red, 1¾″ diameter (rare) 45.00

GN RY—Rectangle logo, American Flag, house, "Free Homes In Central Oregon" on dark blue, 1¾″ diameter (scarce) 30.00

GN RY—Goat atop logo, "See America First: Glacier National Park" red on yellow, 1½″ diameter 15.00

GN RY—"P.P.I.E., 1915," blue and gold on grey with attached blue and gold ribbons, 1¾″ diameter (scarce) 20.00

GN RY—Goat atop streamline diesel train, "The Red River, 1950," orange, green and white, 1¾″ diameter 15.00

GN RY—Logo at center with red, white and blue circles, 1½″ diameter 10.00

GN RY—Goat, "1953 Safety Campaign," red and black on white, 1¼″ diameter 8.00

GN RY—Goat, "Century Of Safety And Progress, 1862-1962," blue and gold on white, 1¾″ diameter 5.00

GN RY—Goat in diesel cab, "You're On The Right Track With Great Northern," yellow background, 2¼″ diameter . 10.00

GN—Set of 17 Safety Campaign pinbacks, 1953-1969, various colors, slogans and goat logos. All 1¼″ diameter . . . 50.00*

Collection of Great Northern safety pinbacks

LV RR—Red flag logo with wreath, "Black Diamond Express," white background, ⅞″ diameter 12.50

JC—"Jersey Central Lines" w/Statue of Liberty logo, white on red, 1¼″ diameter 4.00

MILWAUKEE ROAD—Red logo, "Chicago Railroad Fair, No. 24348," black on white, 1¾″ diameter 10.00

MILWAUKEE ROAD—Indian figure, "Hiawatha Tribe Member," black on yellow, 1¼″ diameter 5.00

NORTHWESTERN LINE—Logo at center with "Alfalfa, The Great Wealth Producer," black on dull yellow, 1¼″ diameter 12.50

NP—"Yellowstone Park Line" logo, red and black on white, 1¾″ diameter 10.00

NP—"Yellowstone Park Line" logo, red and black on white, 1¼″ diameter 5.00

SOO LINE—"75TH ANNIVERSARY, 1883-1958," circle of track w/wheat spray in center, red on white, 2¼″ diameter 15.00

SP—"S.P.R.R. Employees Picnic," Sunset, Ogden & Shasta Routes logo in center, red on white, 1¼″ diameter . . 8.00

UP—Shield logo, "Union Pacific Family," "Service," "War Club," on red background, ⅞″ diameter 7.50

Railroad-related pinback

UP—"Employee Booster's League," white and red on dark blue, oval, ⅝" x 1" 5.00
AMERICAN REFRIGERATOR TRANSIT CO.—GENERAL OFFICES, ST. LOUIS, MO.—"Ship Your Perishable Freight." Depicts large refrigerator car, red, white & blue ribbons with brass balls attached, 2⅛" diameter (scarce)-Complete 30.00*
CHICAGO RAILROAD FAIR—1848-1948, "Wheels A Rolling," pictures streamline diesel train, red, white & blue attached ribbon, 1¾" diameter 15.00
KEYSTONE OVERALLS—"27 Years The Best," multi-colored B of RT emblem in center, 1¼" diameter 5.00
NEW YORK DISPATCH REFRIGERATOR LINES—"National Dispatch," w/picture of refrigerator car, yellow and black on white, 1½" diameter 7.50
RAILROAD CENTENNIAL—"1848-1948, Chicago, Ill." pictures trains and people, black, red and tan on white, 1⅝" diameter 10.00
SHIP BY RAIL—White on black, 1" diameter 2.00

PLAYING CARDS

Railroad playing cards go back to around the turn of the century. The earlier souvenir packs had pictorial scenes on their faces and usually came in a two-piece cardboard slip-case. Subsequent decks with regular face cards came in a standard card stock case with a folding end flap. Packs most in demand and having the higher value are those from the early 1900s, especially decks featuring steam trains, colorful advertising, and interesting logo designs on their backs. Decks with missing or damaged cards, and not in their original box or case, must be discounted in price.

Souvenir pack of years ago

More recent packs

AMTRAK—Logo on backs, original case, recent.......4.00
ACL—Diesel locomotive 525 and palm trees on backs, original case 8.00
B&O—"Capitol Ltd." on backs, original slipcase box, ca. 1926, mint..............45.00
B&O—"National Ltd." on backs, original slipcase box, ca. 1926, mint..............45.00
BAR—Logo against red, white and blue bars on backs, original case, recent..............10.00
BURLINGTON ROUTE—"Parade of Progress" on backs, cello wrapped, mint, recent..............5.00
BURLINGTON ROUTE—Steamlined Zephyr, "America's Distinctive Trains" on backs, original 2-piece box, ca. 1943..22.50
C&A—Red cowgirl on backs, original case, 1903......85.00
C&O—C&O, FFV, "East-West via Washington" on backs, 52 scenes on faces, original slipcase box, ca. 1900.......75.00
C&O—Dble. deck, "Peake--Chessie's Old Man," "Chessie and the Kittens," on gray backs w/CO in corner, orig. 2-pc. box, ca. 1935, mint..............45.00
C&NW—Logo on back, classical figure on wheel, original case, ca. 1935..............37.50
C&NW—Diesel streamliner across "400" on backs, original 2-piece slipbox, ca. 1942..............18.00
C&NW—Yellow diesel locomotive on backs, original 2-piece box, ca. 1948..............15.00
CGW—Gold/black logo on red backs, original case, c. 1950..............15.00
CGW—Blue backs w/white circle engine logo top and bottom, original case, 1940s, mint..............25.00
CM&StP—Souvenir, snowcap mtn. & pines on backs, 52 scenes on faces, original slipcase box, ca. 1915..............47.50
CMStP&P—Souvenir, electric locomotive on backs, 52 scenes on faces, original slipcase box, ca. 1930..............42.00
CMStP&P—"The Olympian" electric on backs, original 2-piece box, ca. 1940..............22.00
CMStP&P—"Hiawatha #1" on backs, original 2-piece box, ca. 1942 ....20.00
CMStP&P—Hiawatha figure on backs, original case, ca. 1965 ....15.00
CO&G—Indian chief on backs, original 2-piece slipcase, ca. 1899, (rare) 150.00
D&RG—Souvenir, train in Royal Gorge on backs, State seal in corners, 52 scenes on faces, original slipcase box, ca. 1922 ....45.00
D&RGW—Souvenir, train in Royal Gorge, suspension bridge on backs, 52 scenes on faces, original slipcase box, ca. 1930s 35.00
DM&I—Logo on backs, Armed Forces insignia, original 2-piece box, 1943..............22.50
GN—Red, white goat logo on backs, original case, ca. 1930s 42.50
GN—Blue, 2 gold/red circles with mountain goat on backs, black logo at feet, ca. 1915..............55.00
GN—Chief Wades-In-The-Water on backs, original case, ca. 1947 ....15.00
GN—Double deck, Chief Wades-In-The-Water, Julia Wades-In-The-Water on backs, original 2-piece box, ca. 1948, mint 30.00

GN—Double deck, Chief Middle Rider, Buckskin Pinto Woman on backs, original 2-piece box, ca. 1951, mint........30.00
GTR—Souvenir, Bonnet girl and roses on backs, 52 scenes on faces, original slipcase box, ca. 1900..............100.00
IC—"Panama Ltd." on backs, original case, ca. 1935, mint 45.00
IC—"Floridan Ltd." on backs, original case, ca. 1935, mint 45.00
IC—Church spires scene on backs, original case, ca. 1968 ....10.00
L&N—"General" and modern diesel on backs, cello wrapped, recent 8.00*
MO-PAC—Double deck, Streamliner "Eagle" against mountain background on backs, 2-piece box, 1950s..............35.00
MO-PAC—"The Sunshine Special" on backs, original case, ca. 1926 ....75.00
MO-PAC—Double deck, Buzz-saw logo on backs, original slipcase, ca. 1932..............36.00
NYC—"20th Century Ltd., Morning on the Mohawk" on backs, orig. box, ca. 1926..............65.00
NICKEL PLATE ROAD—Silver logo on backs, no box or case, ca. 1940s..............15.00
N&W—Double deck, gold logo on black backs, original plush slipcase, mint..............20.00
NP—Double Yellowstone Park Line logo on backs, original case, ca. 1925..............27.50
NP—Red, single Yellowstone Park Line logo on backs, original 2-piece slipcase, ca. 1932..............25.00
NP—Red, single Monad logo on backs, original case, ca. 1957 ....10.00
PRR—Centennial, locomotives, 1846-1946 on backs, original case 22.50
PRR—"Liberty Limited" on stone arch bridge on backs, 2 pc. slipcase, ca. 1920s..............35.00
PRR—Double deck, Keystone logo on backs, 2-piece box, ca. 1960s..............20.00
ROCK ISLAND—Blue filigree design on backs, double logo, orig. case, ca. 1912..............75.00
ROCK ISLAND—Stylized diesel locomotive design on backs, orig. case, recent..............10.00*
ROCK ISLAND—Double deck, black/red logo, "Route Of The Rockets" on backs, original 2-piece box, ca. 1951.....25.00
ROCK ISLAND—Souvenir, orange backs, black globe w/train above and below, 52 scenes on faces, orig. 2 pc. slipcase, ca. 1910 ....55.00
SAL—Souvenir, tan backs w/orange blossoms and Seaboard Rwy. heart logo in center, 52 scenes on faces, orig. 2-pc. slipcase, ca. 1920s..............42.50
SANTA FE—Double deck, diesel trains on backs, original plastic box, recent..............10.00*
SANTA FE—Diesel locomotive #5695 on backs, cello wrapped, recent 6.00
SOO LINE—Green w/gold border and gold logo on backs, original case picturing steam locomotive, ca. 1938..........38.00
SOO LINE—Double deck, Duluth, aerial bridge on backs, original 2-pc. box, 1956..............40.00
SOO LINE—75th Anniversary, 1883-1958, yellow symbol on maroon backs w/logo in corner, orig. case, mint....20.00

SP—Souvenir, Mt. Shasta on backs, 52 scenes on faces, original 2-piece slipcase, ca. 1915 . . . . .50.00

SP—Souvenir, train crossing Great Salt Lake on backs, scenes on faces, orig. 2-piece slipcase, ca. 1926 . . . . 35.00*

SP—Souvenir, streamliner "Daylight" passing mission on backs, 52 scenes on faces, orig. 2-piece slipcase, ca. 1943 .25.00

UP—Centennial 1869-1969, driving Golden Spike on backs, original case 12.00*

UP—Jackson Lake, Teton Range, Wyo., on backs, original case, ca. 1970 . . . . .10.00

WP&Y—Souvenir, blue logo, train on bridge on backs, 52 scenes on faces, original 2-pc. slipcase, ca. 1895 . . . . .110.00

POSTCARDS, STEREO VIEW CARDS

Collecting railroad postcards has become very popular in recent years, with interest in them continuing to rise. Many collect them by categories, such as locomotives, passenger trains, train wrecks, depots, bridges, or various railroad scenes. Besides those put out by the railroads themselves, thousands were made by various manufacturers both here and abroad. In addition to the single postcard, folders and booklets of postcards were issued. Pricing depends on the popularity of the category and the physical condition of the cards. Name trains from the steam era are high on the collector's list. Stereoscopic view cards are also included in this category.

POSTCARDS

AT&SF—View of shops, Topeka, Kansas, unused 4.00

B&O—Locomotive No. 5320, "President Cleveland," exhibited at the Century Of Progress, Chicago, 1933, postmarked 1933 . . . . 2.50

B&O—1933 Century Of Progress, Chicago, set of 15 cards picturing early railroad scenes from paintings, original envelope, mint 35.00

B&O—1827-1927, Centenary Pageant, Baltimore, set of 15 cards picturing locomotives, original envelope, mint 45.00*

Complete set of 1927 B&O Centenary postcards

BURLINGTON ROUTE—Thousand Island Dressing recipe. View of dining car interior and recipe ingredients listed below, unused 6.00

C&O—Wreck of passenger train No. 3 near Hinton, West Virginia, March 12, 1907 . . . . .12.00

C&NW—Interior view of an ultra-modern parlor car on the new streamliner "400," unused .4.00

CGW—Interior view of a standard steel sleeping car, unused 6.00

CGW—Repair shops, Oelwein, Iowa, postmarked 1910 .12.00

CM&StP—View of The Overland Limited passenger train, private mailing card, postmarked 1905 . . . . .20.00

CM&StP—Depot, Aberdeen, South Dakota, postmarked 1909 . . . . 8.00

CM&StP—Souvenir folder of scenes along the route from Butte, Montana to Puget Sound, unused 10.00

D&RG—Souvenir folder of scenes over Soldiers Summit, Utah to Salt Lake City, Utah, unused 10.00

D&SL—Looping the loop of the Continental Divide, Colorado, "Moffat Road," unused 8.00

ERIE—View of Erie Railroad Yards, Hornell, New York, postmarked 1909 . . . . .6.00

GH&S RY—3-part folding postcard picturing train on causeway, Galveston, Tx., 1910 . . . . .15.00*

Three-part folding postcard

GN—Set of 10 cards picturing Blackfeet Indians from paintings by Winold Reiss, original envelope, mint 30.00

GN—Depot scene at Devils Lake, North Dakota, postmarked 1909 . . . . 6.00

GN—View of Lake McDonald, Montana, postmarked 1910 .... 4.00

GN—Souvenir folder of scenes from the Oriental Ltd. enroute St. Paul, Minnesota to Seattle, Washington, dated 1906 .... 12.50

IC—Streamliner, Panama Ltd., against Michigan Ave. skyline, Chicago, mint 5.00

L&N—Railroad bridge across Ohio river between Evansville, Indiana and Henderson, Kentucky, 1952 .... 4.00

LV—The Black Diamond Express between New York, Philadelphia and Buffalo, mint 15.00

MC—View of Niagara Falls from Michigan Central train, mint 15.00

NP—A candy train, model of the North Coast Limited made entirely of sugar, courtesy of the dining car bake shop, mint 15.00

NP—Diesel locomotive 6000 against mountain background, mint 2.50

NP—Souvenir folder of scenes along their western route to Spokane, Washington, ca. 1926, unused 10.00

NYC—New York Central's "Empire State Express," the fastest long distance train in the world, embossed, postmarked 1908 .... 12.50

PRR—Broadway Limited speeding on stone arch bridge, entitled "Speedy and Security," postmarked 1926 ...... 7.50

ROCK ISLAND—Rocky Mountain Rocket at the foot of famous Pikes Peak, mint 3.00

ROCK ISLAND—Train wreck at Gowrie, Iowa, Aug. 15, 1910, postmarked 12.00

SEABOARD—Silver Meteors pass in the scenic highlands of Florida, mint 5.00

SOO LINE—A modern railway, view of passenger train, Twin Cities to Winnipeg, fifteen hours, postmarked 1906 . 15.00

SP—Souvenir folder, The Shasta Route, scenes along their route from San Francisco to Portland, dated 1934, mint . . . 8.00

UP—View of Santa Barbara Mission, California, mint . . . 2.00

UP—Union Pacific Limited train crossing Great Salt Lake, Utah, mint 4.00

UP—Union Pacific streamliner, "City Of Denver," postmarked 1937 .... 3.00

WABASH—The Wabash Banner Limited, operated between St. Louis and Chicago, postmarked 1915 .... 15.00

Miscellaneous railroad postcards

STEREOSCOPIC VIEW CARDS

BCR&N—Passenger train wreck near Waterloo, Iowa, dated May 28, 1899, J.P. King, photographer 22.00

CM&StP—Passenger depot, LaCrosse, Wisconsin, 1879, Elmer & Tenney, Winona, Minnesota, photographers 8.00

D&RG—Passenger train, the Royal Gorge, near Canyon City, Colorado, 1879. Keystone View Company, manufacturers-publishers 10.00

F&PM—Express train at Clare Station, ca. 1875. Goodridge Bros., E. Saginaw, Michigan 25.00

M&StP—"Snowbound" No. 127-The snowed-in engine, 1873. A.L. Mckay, Decorah, Iowa 15.00

MT. WASHINGTON RY—No. 1245, Summit of Mt. Washington, ca. 1885. Kilburn Brothers, Littleton, New Hampshire 10.00

MT. WASHINGTON RY—No. 1825, The Great Trestle, ca. 1885, Kilburn Brothers, Littleton, New Hampshire 10.00

NYNH&H RR—Passenger depot, Springfield, Massachusetts, ca. 1891. E. & H.T. Anthony & Co., New York 15.00

PRR—Engine on the Newport bridge, ca. 1870. Purviance, photographer, Philadelphia 25.00

PRR—Train rounding the famous Horseshoe Curve, Allegheny Mountains, Pennsylvania, ca. 1897. Keystone View Co., Meadville, Pa 15.00

P&O—No. 2088, passenger train at Gates of Crawford Notch. Kilburn Brothers, Littleton, New Hampshire 8.00

P&O—No. 2177, passenger train on bridge, Crawford Notch, New Hampshire. Kilburn Brothers, Littleton, New Hampshire 8.00

W&StP—Roundhouse at Waseca, Minnesota, ca. 1881. Elmer & Tenney, photographers, Winona, Minnesota 30.00

Stereo view cards

RAILROAD POSTMARKS, RPO'S

Covers bearing railroad postmarks are of interest to both the philatelist and the railroadiana collector. Early envelopes were postmarked with the name of the railroad on which they were carried, and these are rare. When railway post office cars were instituted to sort mail enroute, the envelopes bore R.P.O. postmarks. In more recent years, anniversary, first day, and last trip covers were issued to collectors. Many of these had special art work and commemorative railroad postage stamps, known as "cachet covers." There are some who make a specialty of railroad-mail collectibles.

Special note: Many early covers bearing railroad postmarks have high catalog value postage stamps affixed, increasing the price of the cover considerably. Those listed here bear the more common stamps on them, with only nominal catalog value.

COVERS BEARING RAILROAD POSTMARKS

BOSTON & ALBANY RR—ca. 1853 . . . . .30.00
BOSTON & FITCHBURGH RR—ca. 1851 . . . . .40.00
MICH. CENTRAL RR—ca. 1853 . . . . .75.00*
N.Y. & BOSTON STMB. & R.R.R.—ca. 1851 . . . . . . .60.00
PROV. & STONINGTON RR—ca. 1861 . . . . .25.00
SOUTH MINN. RR—ca. 1872 . . . . .35.00
WASHINGTON & PHILA. RR—ca. 1855 . . . . .50.00*
W. & St. PETER R.R.—ca. 1873 . . . . .25.00

Early railroad cancellation covers

COVERS BEARING R.P.O. POSTMARKS

ALAMOSA & DURANGO—R.P.O. TR. 216, Jan. 31, 1951, last
trip San Juan narrow gauge passenger train 3.00
BANGOR & BOS—R.P.O. April 11, 1898 . . . . .8.00
CO. BLUFFS & K.C.—R.P.O. TR 20, Nov. 11, 1934, cachet, first
trip Burlington Zephyr 4.50*
CHI. & FREEPORT—R.P.O. TR 703, Oct. 25, 1948, cachet,
100th Anniversary C&NW System 3.50*
HERON LAKE & PIPESTONE—R.P.O. East, Sept, 30, 1931
 . . . . 5.00
N.Y. & CHI—R.P.O. E.D. TR 51, Dec. 7, 1941, cachet, first trip
streamlined Empire Sate Express 4.00
PITTSBURGH & ST. LOUIS—R.P.O. TR 7, Dec. 15, 1909
 . . . . 6.00
ST. ALBANS & BOSTON—R.P.O. TR 53, Mar. 1, 1894
 . . . . 7.00

RPO cachet covers

ROLLING STOCK RELICS

Since the demise of the Iron Horse, and when railroads stopped running their passenger trains, there has been an increasing interest among rail buffs in preserving relics from the steam locomotive and discontinued rolling stock. Engine bells, headlights, whistles and such are now bringing good prices, along with ornate brass door handle sets, fancy brass luggage racks and wall shelves, ceiling and wall lamps, and so on, from the passenger cars of yesteryear. Many of these items from the vanished Iron Horse and coaches in use during the steam era can still be found today by the diligent collector. Good luck in your search.

AIR BRAKE CONTROL HANDLE—locomotive cab, cast brass
w/steel tension bar, 9½", Westinghouse 20.00
BELL—steam locomotive, cast bronze, iron yoke and stand,
unmarked 750.00*

Steam locomotive bell

Early box-type locomotive headlight

BRAKE WHEEL—cast iron, spoke type, 16" diameter, railroad
marked, pre-1900 . . . . 75.00
DOOR HANDLE SET—coach, 2 pieces, cast brass, ornate design,
early 1900s 50.00
DRUMHEAD—rear observation car, CHICAGO & NORTH-
WESTERN LINE logo at center, NORTHWESTERN
LIMITED, around 26" dia., electric lighted 425.00
DRUMHEAD—Rear observation car, NORTHERN PACIFIC,
NORTH COAST LTD., rectangular, 28¼" x 20½", electric
lighted 375.00
FIRST AID BOX—caboose, metal, 3½" x 8½", wall mounted,
BURLINGTON ROUTE logo 30.00
HAND HOLD—coach, exterior entrance, brass bar, 32" length
. . . . 15.00
HEADLIGHT—locomotive, early, box type, oil burning, made by
M.M. Buck & Co., St. Louis, ca. 1860s 800.00*

HEADLIGHT—steam locomotive, round style, electric, railroad-
marked, Pyle National, ca. 1920s 300.00
HERALD—diesel locomotive, sheet metal, round 24", GREAT
NORTHERN RAILWAY, w/goat at center, red/black/white,
porcelainized enamel 150.00*
HERALD—diesel locomotive, metal, rectangle, 17" x 23", THE
MILWAUKEE ROAD, white letters on red 125.00
LAMP—locomotive cab, kerosene type, complete with font and
globe, Dietz, early 1900s 95.00
LAMP MOUNT BRACKET—caboose, marker lamps, cast iron,
3½" high, pair 20.00
LAMP MOUNT BRACKET—front engine classification, cast
brass, pair, R & L side, with hole for flag mount, 4" high
. . . . 30.00
LETTER DROP CHUTE—mail car, exterior, cast iron hinged
cover, 4" x 7" 75.00

Diesel locomotive herald

Passenger car wall plaque

LINK & PIN COUPLING SET—2 pieces, heavy cast iron, oval
4½″ x 13″, pin 13¾″ long, UP RR, ca. 1880s....65.00
MAIL POUCH—Express car, canvas and leather trim, black sten-
cilled letters RAILWAY EXPRESS AGENCY, with serial
number....................................40.00
NUMBER PLATE—front of steam engine, cast brass, round,
8½″, BALDWIN LOCOMOTIVE WORKS, PHILADELPHIA,
U.S.A., digits in center.....................300.00
LUGGAGE RACK—coach, fancy cast brass w/steel bottom grill,
12″ x 36″...................................250.00
PLAQUE—coach, stainless steel, rectangle, 5½″ x 21″, yellow
and black enamel letters "S P & S".............55.00
PLAQUE—coach, brass, rectangle, 4″ x 12″, raised letters
"PASSENGERS NOT ALLOWED TO STAND ON THE
PLATFORM"..................................35.00
PLAQUE—passenger car wall decor, MILWAUKEE ROAD,
Hiawatha Indian figure cut-out, aluminum, 11½″ x 19″, oval,
½″ thick...................................150.00*
RUG—parlor car, wool, green and black floral design on red, large
G.N.RY. goat logo in center, 27″ x 46″........200.00*
SEAL—Express car, metal strip 8¼″ long with ball end, embossed
"REA EXP." and serial number, unused..........2.00
SEAL—box car, metal strip 8¼″ long with ball end embossed
with railroad initials and serial number, unused......4.00
SIGN—passenger car entrance, "WATCH YOUR STEP," 3¼″
x 21″, porcelainized steel, white letters on black...35.00
SIGN—sleeping car, stainless, rectangle, 3¼″ x 5″, white letters
on black, "TO GET IN OR OUT OF UPPER BERTH
PLEASE USE THE LADDER".................35.00*
SOAP HOLDER—coach, wall type, brass, ornate, early.20.00
SPEED RESTRICTION PLAQUE—locomotive, brass, 1¾″ x
5¼″, cast letters, "70 MPH MAXIMUM PERMISSIBLE
LOCOMOTIVE SPEED".....................30.00
STEP STOOL—passenger car, metal, embossed "GREAT
NORTHERN" front side, Morton Mfg. Co., Chgo..185.00

Parlor car rug

Sleeping car wall sign

STEP STOOL—passenger car, metal, embossed with NORTHERN PACIFIC Monad logo front and back.......150.00*
STEP STOOL—passenger car, metal, embossed with SOO LINE logo front, Morton Mfg. Co., Chgo..............200.00
STEP STOOL—passenger car, metal, embossed "UNION PACIFIC" across front, Morton Mfg. Co., Chgo...135.00
STEP STOOL—Pullman, metal, embossed "PULLMAN" both sides, made by Utica......................150.00
STEP LADDER—sleeping car, wood, height 36″, hinged back, carpeted treads, railroad-marked.................85.00

Passenger car step stool

STOVE—caboose, cast iron, coal burning, lids on top, fire chamber, ash pan bottom, small size, approx. 28″ tall, railroad-marked....................................500.00
TICKET HOLDER—coach, wall mount type, brass, ornate shape, 1⅜″ x 2″, incised "TICKET" and RR initials......15.00
TRUST PLATE—NP, cast aluminum, 5″ x 12″, "NORTHERN PACIFIC RAILWAY, EQUIPMENT TRUST OF 1966, FIRST NATIONAL CITY BANK, TRUSTEE, OWNER, LESSOR"
....25.00
TRUST PLATE—C&NW, cast iron, 6½″ x 16″, "THE NORTHERN TRUST COMPANY, TRUSTEE, OWNER AND LESSOR, CHICAGO AND NORTHWESTERN RY. CO., THIRD EQUIP. TRUST OF 1953".............35.00
TRUST PLATE—CB&Q, cast aluminum, 5¼″ x 13½″, "CHICAGO BURLINGTON & QUINCY RAILROAD EQUIPMENT TRUST NO. 3 of 1965, THE NORTHERN TRUST COMPANY, TRUSTEE, OWNER AND LESSOR".. 25.00*

Cast aluminum trust plate

WALL LAMP—Pullman berth, electric, brass, complete with shade 65.00
WALL SHELF—coach, all brass, rectangular with rounded front corners, grilled, 6½″ x 27″....................75.00
WHISTLE—caboose, back-up, all brass with lever, 8″ tall, Sherburn Co., ca. 1910..........................35.00
WHISTLE—steam locomotive, brass, triple chamber chime, 14″ tall to acorn finial, Buckeye Brass Works, Dayton, Ohio
....200.00
WHISTLE—steam locomotive, brass, single chamber, chime, 15″ tall to final, Powell's.......................150.00
WHISTLE—locomotive cab, cast brass, "peanut" whistle, 3″ tall, air operated, engineer overspeed warning.........18.00
WINDOW SASH LOCK—coach, brass, spring-action type with finger grips...................................8.00

SHEET MUSIC

Many pieces of sheet music have been published pertaining to the railroads over the years. "Casey Jones, The Brave Engineer," is a classic example. Especially desirable are those picturing the train on their colorful covers. Fine copies from the early 1900s are in demand, steadily increasing in price. Some sheet music was published exclusively for the railroad or dedicated to the Brotherhoods, and these are preferred by the more serious railroadiana collector.

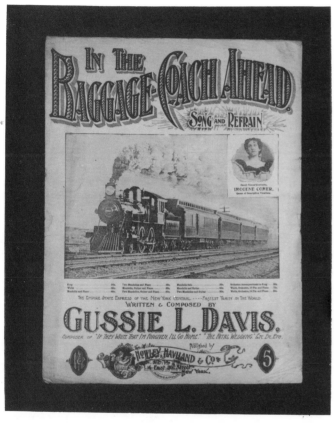

Public railroad sheet music

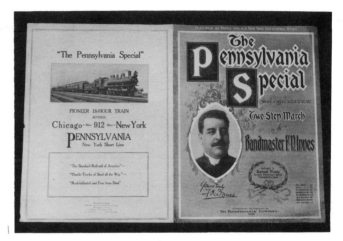

Authentic railroad sheet music

"CASEY JONES, THE BRAVE ENGINEER"—words & music by Seibert and Newton, Southern California Music Co., Los Angeles, 1909. Cover shows front end of locomotive with 2 men in cab 15.00

"HAIL THE BALTIMORE & OHIO"—centenary march, pub. for B&O by Walter Goodwin, Inc., N.Y., 1927. The "President Washington" locomotive is on the front cover 20.00

"IN THE BAGGAGE COACH AHEAD"—song & refrain, Gussie L. Davis, pub. by Howley, Haviland Co., N.Y., 1896. "Empire State Express" on cover 25.00*

"I'VE BEEN WORKING ON THE RAILROAD"—words & music, Calumet Music Co., Chgo., 1935. Man waving to train on cover 8.00

"MAKE THAT ENGINE STOP AT LOUISVILLE"—words & music by Lewis & Meyer, pub. by Geo. W. Myer Music Co., N.Y., 1914. Cover has a Louisville & Nashville RR train 10.00

"MY DAD'S THE ENGINEER"—song & chorus by Chas. Graham, pub. by Henry J. Wehman, 1895. Cover depicts girl seated in coach pass. train w/her Dad at the throttle 27.50

"PULLMAN PORTER'S PARADE"—words & music, Maurice Abrahams Music Co., N.Y., 1913. Cover shows porters marching 12.00

"RAILROAD RAG"—words & music Nat Vincent, Ed Bimberg, Head Music Pub. Co., N.Y., 1911. Engine on cover . 10.00

"SONG OF THE GREAT BIG BAKED POTATO"—published for the Northern Pacific Railroad Dining Car Dept., 1912. Cover pictures logos & baked potato 35.00

"SUNSET LIMITED"—march by Henry Bartell, pub. McKinley Music Co., Chicago, 1910. Cover has pass. train speeding in-to the setting sun 6.00

"THE BUFFALO FLYER"—march two-step by Harry Lincoln, pub. Vandersloot Music Co., Williamsport, Pa., 1904. Speeding pass. train at night depicted on cover 12.50

"THE CHICAGO EXPRESS"—march two-step by Percy Wenrich, McKinley Music Co., Chgo., 1905. Passenger train on cover 8.50

"THE MIDNIGHT FLYER"—march two-step, by E.T. Paull, pub. by E.T. Paull Music Co., N.Y., 1903. Lithographed scene of train leaving depot at night 22.50

"THE PENNSYLVANIA SPECIAL"—two-step march by Band-master F.N. Innes, pub. by the Pennsylvania Co., 1905. Back cover has photo of "The Pennsylvania Special" passenger train 25.00*

"THE WESTERN FLYER"—march two-step, by Paul Morton, pub. McKinley Music Co., Chgo., 1919. Pass. train rounding curve of track on cover 5.00

"WHERE DO YOU WORK-A JOHN?-DELAWARE LACKA-WAN"—Ernie Krickett, Shapiro Bernstein Music Pub. Co., N.Y., 1926. Cover depicts two men on hand-car 18.00

"WHEN THAT MIDNIGHT CHOO CHOO LEAVES FOR ALA-BAM"—by Irving Berlin, Ted Snyder Co. Music Publishers, N.Y., 1912. Cover depicts passenger train at night . . 10.00

SIGNS

Ever since the railroads got out of the passenger train business, the collecting of signs that once adorned the walls of depots has proliferated. Of special interest are the various Express Company and Telegraph Company signs that hung on the outside walls of small town depots. Many were two-sided, white and blue porcelainized metal signs that could be read from both ends of the station platform. Express Company signs were also used on baggage carts and delivery trucks. Express Company call card signs were distributed to local merchants to be displayed in the front window of their stores attracting the attention of the Express Company driver to stop and make a parcel pick-up.

Every depot had signs located at opposite ends of the building with the name of the station shown on them. The railroad serving the line also had their official logo signs posted on the outside walls of the depot. All of these miscellaneous exterior and interior signs from the vanished depots are bringing high prices today. Reproductions are being made, so be wary!

"ADAMS EXPRESS CO.-MONEY ORDERS SOLD HERE."—depot exterior, one sided, 3″ x 30″, red herald one end, white letters on green, porcelainized steel, ca. 1900......150.00

"AIR EXPRESS-DIVISION RAILWAY EXPRESS AGENCY, INC."—delivery trucks, one-sided diamond shape, 8″ x 8″, white wings and letters on red, porcelainized steel, 2 grommet holes 75.00

"AMERICAN EXPRESS CO."—depot exterior, two-sided, porcelainized steel, 13″ x 17″, "Money Orders, Foreign Drafts, Traveler's Cheques, Letters of Credit, Telegraphic Transfers," white on blue, dated 1914......................250.00

"AMERICAN RAILWAY EXPRESS"—call card, diamond shape, two-sided, 14″ x 14″, red, white and green, heavy cardboard with metal rims, grommeted hole at top, ca. 1920s.......100.00*

Cardboard call sign

"BURLINGTON ROUTE"—depot exterior logo, mounted flush, rectangular, 21″ x 27″, white, black and red, heavy steel, stamped "CB&Q RR" on back side......................150.00

"DEER CREEK"—depot exterior station name sign, mounted flush, 12″ x 66″ long, black on white, heavy steel.....50.00

GREAT NORTHERN—"WAITING ROOM," depot interior, 10″ x 26″, wood, white letters on black...............35.00

NORTHERN PACIFIC—"NOTICE-The Value Of All Baggage Must Be Declared In Writing," depot interior, 10″ x 13″, cardboard, 1948.....................................15.00

NORTHERN PACIFIC—"PARCEL CHECK ROOM Inquire At Ticket Window," depot interior, 7″ x 11″, cardboard, 1946 ....15.00

"PUBLIC TELEPHONE"—depot exterior, hanging, two-sided, 18″ x 18″, bell in center, blue on white, porcelainized steel 45.00

RAILWAY EXPRESS AGENCY—"PACKAGES RECEIVED HERE", depot exterior, hanging, two-sided, 15″ x 18″, red diamond on white, black letters at bottom, porcelainized steel 75.00

"RAILWAY EXPRESS AGENCY"—call card, diamond shape, two sided, 14″ x 14″, white letters on red, heavy cardboard with metal rims, grommeted hole at top, 1950s................50.00

"RAILWAY EXPRESS AGENCY"—depot exterior, mounted flush, one-sided, 11½″ x 72″ long, yellow letters on black, porcelainized steel.............................125.00

"RAILWAY EXPRESS AGENCY"—baggage cart, one-sided, diamond shape, 14″ x 14″, white, black and red, porcelainized steel, 1950s...30.00

"RAILWAY EXPRESS AGENCY"—depot interior, 13¼″ x 19¼″, lithographed tin. Picture of locomotive, men unloading Express car, truck arriving. Black letters "Fast Dependable Through Service" on white background, 1930s......250.00*

"REA EXPRESS"—depot exterior, 3¾″ x 60″, white letters on green, porcelainized steel........................20.00

"REA EXPRESS"—baggage cart, one-sided, diamond shape, 12″ x 12″, white on red, porcelainized metal, 2 grommeted holes 22.00

"REA EXPRESS"—call card, two-sided, diamond shape, 14″ x 14″, white on red, fiberglass. Brass grommeted hanging hole at top. Final issue................................15.00

"UNION PACIFIC SYSTEM-TICKETS FOR CHILDREN"—"Under the Law, children 5 years old and under 12 must pay Half Fare; 12 years or over, Full Fare," depot interior, 8″ x 10″, white and blue porcelainized steel, 1930s................100.00*

Lithographed tin sign

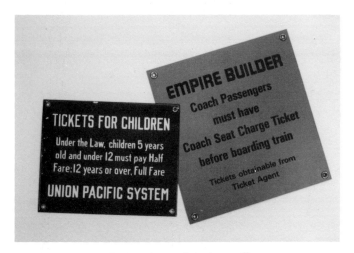

Depot signs - interior wall

"WELLS FARGO & CO. EXPRESS"—call card, diamond shape, two-sided, 14″ x 14″, black, white and red, heavy cardboard with metal rims, grommeted hole at top, ca. 1920s 250.00

"WESTERN UNION"—depot exterior, two-sided porcelainized metal, 11″ x 17″, "TELEGRAPH HERE," white on blue, "WESTERN UNION" in black on yellow slanting below 85.00

"WESTERN UNION TELEGRAPH AND CABLE"—depot exterior, hanging, two-sided, 12″ x 24″, white on blue, porcelainized steel 135.00

"WESTERN UNION TELEGRAPH AND CABLE OFFICE"—depot exterior door, mounted flush, one-sided, 4″ x 9″, white on blue, porcelainized steel, 1930s 45.00

"WESTERN UNION TELEGRAPH AND CABLE"—depot exterior, hanging, two-sided, 11″ x 16″, globe center, white on dark blue, porcelainized steel 150.00*

"WESTERN UNION TELEGRAMS"—depot exterior, hanging, two-sided, 10″ x 17″ white on dark blue, porcelainized steel 75.00

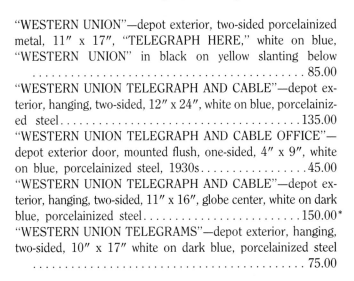

Two-sided sign - exterior depot

SMOKING ACCESSORIES

Millions of book matches were handed out freely by the railroads, having their logos, name trains, and colorful advertising printed on the covers. Those from the steam era are especially desirable and are worth more. Countless numbers of ashtrays were used on the diners, smoking and parlor cars, and in the railroads ticket offices and depots. These were made of glass, ceramic, and metal, in various shapes and sizes, with the railroad's logo prominently displayed. The older ashtrays are more in demand and priced higher. Note: Reproduction heavy glass ashtrays with authentic railroad heralds on them are being made for the hobby trade, and these are not to be confused with the genuine railroad-issued ashtrays.

The small, pocket-type cigarette lighters with the railroad's name or logo on them are collectible and moderately priced. Those from several decades past sell for more. The railroad-marked spittoons or cuspidors from the early days are also sought after by collectors. The all-brass cuspidor is the most popular and brings a higher price. Miscellaneous items are listed at the end.

ASHTRAYS (BS-backstamped)

ALTON—glass, 3½″ square, triangle logo with "The Alton Railroad Company" in red and white on bottom....15.00

BN—glass, 8-sided, 5″ x 5″, BN logo with "Burlington Northern" in green on bottom..........................5.00

C&O—china, Syracuse, round, 4″ diameter, blue and yellow pinstripes with Chessie kitten on bottom..........35.00

C&O—china, Buffalo, white, rectangular, 3¼″ x 7¼″, Geo. Washington silhouette inside, "The Geo. Washington R.R. Chesapeake & Ohio Lines," w/black stripe on front side 85.00

CGW—glass, round with 5 protruding rests, 3¼″ dia., fluted sides, "Chicago Great Western Ry." on bottom..........18.00*

Miscellaneous glass ashtrays

CNW—ceramic, 5″ x 5″, irreg. base with standing figure of traveler owl, inscribed "Travel Wise-Chicago & Northwestern Lines," between rests, 1941...........................75.00*

Novelty ashtrays - composition

CNW—ceramic, 5″ x 5″ irreg. base with standing figure of trainman owl inscribed "Freight Wise-Chicago & Northwestern Lines" between rests, 1941 (scarce)..............75.00*

CLINCHFIELD—china, no BS, white, round 5″ diameter, dble end steam locomotive on bottom, "Clinchfield Railroad Co." and advertising copy in gold around edge.........30.00

CLINCHFIELD—china, Royal, white, round 5¼″ diameter, dble end diesel locomotive with "Clinchfield Railroad" in brown on bottom.....................................25.00

COTTON BELT ROUTE—copper, round 3½″ diameter, Cotton Belt Route logo embossed on bottom w/raised designs between rests.....................................20.00

GN—china, Syracuse, white, round 4″ diameter, silhouette goat on mountain top w/evergreens in border, BS, Great Northern Railroad....................................125.00

GN—china, Syracuse, white, round 4″ diameter, 3 flowers in center, BS. Great Northern Ry.................75.00

GN—porcelain, black, round 4″ diameter, Great Northern, old goat logo in bottom, BS, "Genuine P & S porcelain"45.00

GN—porcelain, Ekstrand, rose, round 4¼″ diameter, Great Northern Railway, mountain goat logo on white in bottom, BS, "SNUF-A-RETTE" w/history....................35.00

GN—plastic, black, round, 4½″ diameter, 4 white goat logos around sides, BS, "The Derby No. 925"..........18.00

GN—glass, round, 4″ diameter, entwined GN letters in white on bottom.....................................15.00

M&StL—glass, 3½″ square, red/black logo on bottom.18.00*

M&STL—ceramic, blue, round, 5½″ diameter, "The Peoria Gateway Line" logo embossed on bottom, "The Minneapolis & St. Louis Railroad" in white around outside edge.55.00

NP—glass, 3½″ square, black/red Yellowstone Park Line logo on bottom....................................15.00

NP—glass, 4½″ square, black/red Yellowstone Park Line logo on bottom....................................20.00

NP—glass, 4½″ square, black/red NP Monad logo on bottom 12.00

NP—glass, 8-sided, 5″ x 5″, black/red NP Monad logo on bottom 18.00*

PULLMAN—bakelite, brown, round, 5½″ diameter, "The Pullman Company" raised between rests. Made by Samul Lewis Co., N.Y.....................................15.00

ROCK ISLAND—glass, 4¼″ square, red logo on bottom 12.00*

SOO LINE—glass, 4″ square, red/white logo on bottom 15.00

SOO LINE—glass, blue, round, 4½″, 3 red/white decal logos around edge, "Nomesser, Patt. Applied For" on bottom 25.00*

SOO LINE—metal, black finish, round, 6″, red logo on pearlized disc in center circle.....................30.00

SR—copper, round, 5½″, S.R. logo embossed on bottom. "Southern Railway System-The Southern Serves The South" around edge.................................22.50

T&P—ceramic, Hall, blue, oval, 4 x 5½″, gold diamond logo both sides of center holder........................65.00

UP—glass, blue, round, 4¼″ diameter, "Union Pacific Railroad, Sun Valley Idaho, Utah Parks Co." in red on white at bottom (also found in clear, green and amber)...........12.00

BOOK MATCHES (Complete with matches unless otherwise noted)

ACL—Logo, list of name trains, silver printing on purple 1.50

AA—Flag logo, "Double A Service," red and blue printing on white 1.00

B&O—Gold logo on blue, list of name trains backside (cover only) 1.50

BURLINGTON ROUTE—Zephyr, list of name trains on silver 1.75

CGW—Gold logo front, map backside on red background 3.00

CMStP&P—Red logo, Hiawatha streamliner #1 on black and grey 2.00

CPR—Beaver atop red shield logo, gold background 1.35

ERIE—Logo and diesel streamliner, yellow printing on blue (cover only) 1.00

FRISCO LINES—Black logo on yellow against red stripes 1.00

GN—Logo and Indian, "Route Of The Empire Builder" on white background 2.00

GB&W—Red logo and diesel on black with yellow lines (cover only) 1.00

IC—Diamond logo and black steam locomotive on green and gold 2.50

LACKAWANNA—Gold logo, "Route of Phoebe Snow" on maroon 1.00

M&StL—Cartoon showing brakeman catching boxcar w/slogan "Get A Grip On Safety," red/black on white 2.50

MO-PAC—Hounddog, route of the Eagles logo, yellow background 2.00

NICKEL PLATE ROAD—Logo, "NKP" on map, blue printing on cream 1.25

NP—Yellowstone Park Line logo on red background, "Main Street Of The Northwest" 1.50

NYC—Red logo frontside, trains "Travel & Ship By Dependable Rail" backside, on grey 1.50

NYO&W—W logo, white printing on dark blue (cover only) 1.00

N&W—Streamline steam train, Pocahantas and Cavalier, blue background 2.00

PRR—1846-1946, 100 year emblem, gold on maroon . . . 2.00

QUANAH ROUTE—Logo, Indian chief, purple and white (cover only) 1.50

RIO GRANDE—Logo and advertising, black printing on red (cover only) 1.00

SOO LINE—Red logo on dark blue both sides 2.00

SP—Stylized daylight streamliner on yellow 1.75

T&P—Red logo on green background (cover only) 1.50

WABASH—Red flag logo on dark blue (cover only) 1.50

PAX OF SIX, CELLO WRAPPED

GN—White covers with black/red goat logo and "Great For Freight" at bottom 6.00

GN—Blue covers with modern white goat logo and "Great Northern" at bottom 6.00

NP—Red covers with black/red logo and "Main Street Of The Northwest" at bottom, "Vista Dome North Coast Limited" logo and dome car on back cover 9.00

ROCK ISLAND—Red covers with black/white logo 3.00

SANTA FE—Dark blue covers with white Santa Fe cross logo 12.00

UNION PACIFIC—Red covers with gold shield logo. Other side has "Union Pacific Railroad" in gold letters 3.00

WM—White cover with Western Maryland Railway, logo in red, other side has a red diesel loco, #7447 . . . . 3.00

CARDBOARD BOXES OF BOOK MATCHES (full count)

CNW—28 books, green covers, "Route Of The '400' Streamliner Fleet And Western Streamliners" w/2 diesels on front cover. Back has colored logo, 1940s (28 @ 1.25 ea.) 35.00*

NYC—50 books, red/white/blue covers, logo and Mercury figure on front cover. Back has the "James Whitcomb Riley" streamliner pictured, 1940s (50 @ 1.00 ea.) 50.00

NYC—50 books, white covers, logo and "Empire State Express" on front cover. Back has picture of the new steam Empire State Express, 1940s (50 @ 1.00 ea.) 50.00

ROCK ISLAND—25 books, red covers, black/red logo both sides (25 @ .50 ea.) 12.50

SANTA FE—50 books, white covers, black Santa Fe logo with Indian boy on both sides (50 @ .25 ea.) 12.50

Book matches

CIGARETTE LIGHTERS

A&S—Locomotive, logo, Agent's name, black/red on silver, Rolex
. . . . .22.00
C&NW—Black/red logo on silver, Zippo 15.00
CM&StP—White logo and Indian figure on red, Warren
. . . . .10.00
FRISCO—Logo, map of system, gold on red, Vulcan . .18.00
GN—Logo, diesel train, red/black on silver, "GN" 15.00*
M&StL—Black/red logo on silver, Zippo 30.00
MN&S—Red logo on silver, Halco 30.00
SOO LINE—Logo both sides, white on maroon, Warren
. . . . .12.00
SANTA FE—Chico Indian boy, logo, red on gold, WindMaster
. . . . .8.00
UP—Raised shield logo on silver, Barlow 8.00

Front and back of cigarette lighter

CUSPIDORS

MO-PAC—Metal, white enamel with black "MO-PAC" on side rim,
7¼″ top dia., 5″ tall 110.00
N&W—Porcelainized cast iron, "N & W" raised on outside, 8½″
top dia., 5″ tall 105.00
PULLMAN—Nickel finish on brass, "THE PULLMAN CO."
stamped on bottom, 7″ dia., 3″ tall 65.00
PULLMAN—Nickel finish on brass, "PULLMAN" incised on cast
iron bottom, 8½″ dia., 7″ tall 100.00
SP—White porcelainized steel w/blue "S.P.CO." on inside rim,
8″ top dia., 5″ tall 75.00
SOO LINE—Brass, raised logo on cast iron bottom, 9″ top dia.,
7½″ tall 175.00*
SOO LINE—Dark blue porcelainized steel with "SOO LINE" in
light blue on inside white rim, 8½″ top dia., 5″ tall
. . . . .95.00*
UP—Green porcelainized steel, black "UNION PACIFIC" on in-
side rim, 8″ top dia., 5″ tall .85.00

Brass and porcelainized steel cuspidors

MISCELLANEOUS (YPL-Yellowstone Park Lines)

CIGAR BAND—Northern Pacific, YPL logo on gold 5.00
CIGAR BAND—Southern Pacific, sunset logo on gold . .5.00
CIGAR BOX—Burlington Route, wood, 2½″ x 5½″ x 8″, logo
on cover 35.00*
CIGAR BOX—The Northwestern Line, wood, 1½″ x 5″ x 8¾″,
logo on cover 30.00
CIGAR BOX—Northern Pacific, wood, 1½″ x 6¼″ x 8½″,
"Carabana" NP logo on inside cover 25.00*
CIGAR BOX—PRR, wood, 2″ x 6″ x 9¼″, "Crooks," streamliner
rounding Horse Shoe Curve on cover 20.00
CIGAR BOX—Soo Line, wood, 2¼″ x5″ x 7¾″, "Soo Line" on
cover, picture of train on inside 45.00
CIGARETTE CASE—Northern Pacific, tin, black enamel, 1″ x
2″ x 3″, YPL logo and "Route Of The North Coast Limited"
and "First Of The Northern Transcontinentals" in white
. . . . .35.00

Railroad cigar boxes

FLOOR STAND ASHTRAY—CNW, cast iron and steel, 26″ black/chrome finish, round top tray 15″ dia., chrome logo on base 175.00

SAFETY MATCHES—Pullman, blue/white cardboard box, ¾″ x 1½″ x 2¼″, wood stick matches inside, Pullman car logo on cover, Diamond Match Co 5.00

SAFETY MATCHES—Union Pacific, white cardboard box, ½″ x 1⅜″ x 2″, wood stick matches inside, shield logo and "We Can Handle It" on cover 1.00

STATIONERY ITEMS

There are numerous items that the collector can search for in this category. Pencils and pens carrying railroad logos, blotters featuring vacation spots and name passenger trains, rulers with interesting advertising slogans, scratch pads, letterheads and envelopes, etc.; all were once produced in large quantities and widely distributed. Railroad marked stationery items are now getting scarce and prices on them are on the rise.

BALL POINT PENS

BN—Black/white, logo, "Burlington Northern" and ad slogan in green on white, Tucker 1.00

DM&IR—Maroon/gold, "D.M. & I.R." and "Marshalling Yard Keenan, 10/23/76" in maroon on gold, Readyriter . . 12.00

GN—White, modern goat logo and "Great Northern" in blue, Sheaffer 2.00

GN—Black/silver, Rocky goat logo, and "Great For Freight, Great For Travel, Great Northern Railway" in black on silver, Autopoint 8.00

MILWAUKEE ROAD—Black/gold, canted box logo in yellow on black, Readyriter 4.00

NP—Two-tone green, Monad logo and "Northern Pacific Railway Company, St. Paul, Minn." in black on light green, Readyriter 5.00

SOO LINE—Black, w/gold bands at clip, logo and "Soo Line Railroad" in gold on black, Wings 10.00

PEN POINTS

CGW RY—steel pen point with wood holder, cork grip . 10.00

GN RY—steel pen point with wood holder 6.00

M&STL RR—steel pen point with wood holder, cork grip 10.00

NYNH&H RR—steel pen point, without holder 3.00

N&W RY—steel pen point, without holder 3.00

PENCILS (wood, with graphite leads-unsharpened)

ACL—"Atlantic Coast Line," gold printing on dark brown, round, No. 2, eraser 2.50

BN—"Burlington Northern-Safety & Courtesy Pays," white printing on green, hexagon, No.1, eraser 35

CB&Q—"Burlington Lines-Everywhere West," black printing on yellow, hexagon, No. 2, eraser 2.50

CGW—"C.G.W.RY.," gold printing on green, hexagon, No. 2 "Bondexed lead," eraser 5.00

CStPM&O—"C.ST.P.M. & O.RY." gold printing on maroon, round, No. 2, no eraser 4.00

C&NW—"C. & N.W. RY. CO.," white printing on maroon, round, No. 2, no eraser 2.50

C&O—"The Chesapeake and Ohio Railway Company," black on chrome yellow, hexagon, no eraser 35

M&StL—"M. & St.L.Ry Co.," gold printing on black, round, No. 1, no eraser 5.00

MKT—"M-K-T-Katy Lines-The Bluebonnet, The Texas Special," red/blue printing on yellow, hexagon, eraser 2.00

MP—"Missouri Pacific Lines," white printing on brown, hexagon, No. 2, eraser 1.00

MILWAUKEE—Red logo, "Safety First, Always Be Careful, Prevent Accidents" black printing on yellow, round, eraser 3.00

NC&StL—"N.C. & ST.L. RWY.-To and From Dixielands," green printing on yellow, hexagon, No. 2, eraser.........2.00

NP—"Northern Pacific Ry.-Courteous-Friendly", silver printing on maroon, round, No. 1, no eraser.............2.00

REA—"Railway Express Agency," silver printing on red, round, No. 3, no eraser...................................1.50

RI—"Rock Island Lines," black printing on red, round, No. 2, no eraser....................................1.00

SOO LINE—"Friendliness is a Soo Line Tradition," white printing on black, round, No.2, no eraser.............3.50

UP—"Union Pacific Railroad,-If Damage Is Low Business Will Grow," red printing on yellow, hexagon, No. 3, eraser..35

WABASH—"Follow The Flag-logo, "Wabash Railroad" blue letters on white, round, fat pencil, eraser...........10.00

PENCILS, MECHANICAL

C&NW—"Chicago and North Western Line—Route of The '400,' The Challengers, The Streamliners" green printing on yellow, green ends, Redipoint.........................9.50*

FRISCO—Gold logo and printing on black, gold ends, Ritepoint 10.00

GN—Red/blue goat logo on pearlized, black ends, no manufacturer 15.00*

MILWAUKEE—Hiawatha steam train, red logo, "Route Of The Hiawathas," "Friendliness is a MILWAUKEE ROAD Tradition," pearlized, Quickpoint...................18.00

M&STL—"The Minneapolis & St. Louis Railway," diesel freight on white, black ends, Redipoint................20.00

MO-PAC—Red logo w/steam train, "It's 70 in the SUNSHINE when it's 100 in the SHADE," black on pearlized, Quickpoint 18.00

PULLMAN—"Pullman, Standard Car Mfg. Co., World's Largest Builders of Railroad Cars," white printing on maroon, black ends, Autopoint.............................8.00*

RIO GRANDE—logo, "Rio Grande, The Direct General Transcontinental Route," black printing on red arrow, pearlized, no manufacturer 15.00

ROCK ISLAND—Rocket streamliner, 2 red logos, "Travel and Ship Route of the ROCKETS," red/black printing on pearlized, no manufacturer.......................15.00*

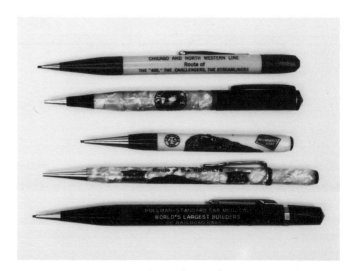

Mechanical pencils

SAL—"Seaboard Airline Railway—Completely Air-Conditioned Trains," black printing on cream, black ends, Scripto 10.00

SOO LINE—Red logo, "Soo Line Service Satisfies" red printing on pearlized, Quickpoint.......................18.00

UP—Boxed pen/pencil set, logo on clips, Papermate...15.00

RULERS

C&NW—15″ wood, logos front, diesel trains back, 1940s 12.00*

CGW—12″ plastic, logo at center, black printing on white 10.00

CGW—12″ wood, railroad name and advertising both sides, 1930s 20.00*

GM&O—12″ plastic, logos, diesel freight, map, red & black printing on white................................5.00*

GN-8″ celluloid on tin, logo, 1931 calendar, black printing on white......................................15.00

KCS—15″ wood, "Port Arthur Route" front, "Straight As The Crow Flies" map backside, 1903 (rare)...........35.00*

M&StL—12″ enameled tin, logo and advertising, black/red printing on white................................10.00*

SOO LINE—12″ enameled tin, logo, map, red printing on white 7.50

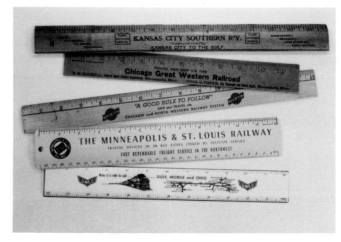

Wood, tin and plastic rulers

BLOTTERS

C&NW—Logo, "The Train For Comfort Is The North-Western Limited," 4″ x 9″, ca. 1905....................20.00

CGW—Black logo and steam train, lists 7 name trains with fares, orange borders, 3¾″ x 8¾″, March, 1931........15.00

CStP&KC—Iron horse with wings, galloping down track, "Time Reduced to 13½″ hours to and from Chicago, St. Paul and Minneapolis" in red on banner, 4″ x 9″, ca. 1889..30.00

CStPM&O—Fireman shoveling coal in engine cab, "The North-Western Line" logo, blue on white, ca. 1895......25.00

GN—Picture of Chief Two Guns White Calf, "Glacier National Park," "The New Empire Builder-Great Northern," 4″ x 9″, 1932...10.00

MILWAUKEE—Logo, "1933—A Century Of Progress," "Chicago! Travel by Train," 3¼″ x 6¼″,...................5.00

MILWAUKEE—Logo and steam train, "The Pioneer Limited," lists arrival & departure times Twin Cities-Chicago, 3¼″ x 6¼″, 1930s...5.00

MILWAUKEE—Logo, "To Chicago—THE SIOUX" w/steam train in center, 3¼″ x 6¼″, 1930s...................5.00

NYC—3 round pictures, LaSalle St. Station, Chicago, Grand Central Station, N.Y., and Twentieth Century Limited center, 4¼″ x 9½″, 1930.................................8.00*

N&W—Colorful wharf scene, "1838-A Century Of Service-1938", 3 calendar months, 4″ x 9″, 1938...............6.00*

NP—Picture of baked potato, "Famous For Good Food—the Streamlined North Coast Limited." 3¾″ x 8½″, 1930s 18.00*

Miscellaneous ink blotters

ROCK ISLAND—Black logo and steam train, arrival & departure times Memphis to Hot Springs National Park, 4″ x 9″, 1930s..8.00

SP—Large map of system, 3 calendar months, 1926, green/tan, 4″ x 9″..10.00

UP—Pictures of Grand Canyon, Zion and Bryce Canyon National Parks in color, reached from Cedar City, Utah via UNION PACIFIC, 4″ x 9″, 1930s.....................5.00*

WABASH—Logo, lady in coach, "The Luxurious Way to Chicago, Wabash Banner Blue Limited," 3½″ x 6½″, 1920s.15.00*

STATIONERY—Tourist

BURLINGTON—sheet of paper and envelope, "Denver Zephyr" small size....................................2.00

GN—sheet of paper and envelope, "The Oriental Limited" small size..2.50

GN—"TRAVEL SERVICE," logo and view of Lake St. Mary, Glacier National Park across top, 8½″ x 11″.......2.00

IC—envelope, standard size, Illinois Central diesel, logo.1.00

LV—envelope, business size, "Lehigh Valley Railroad Co." 1.25

MILWAUKEE ROAD—sheet of paper and envelope, "Route Of The Hiawathas," small size.....................2.00

ROCK ISLAND—sheet of paper and envelope, "Route Of The Rockets," small size...........................2.00

SANTA FE—sheet of paper and envelope, "The Chief Way," small size..2.00

MISCELLANEOUS

D&RGW—scratch pad, picture of diesel freight in Rocky Mountains.....................................4.00

EJ&E RY—scratch pad holder, 5½″ x 9″, steel, logo and "Elgin, Joliet & Eastern Railway" in green on white enamel clip 18.00

FRISCO—scratch pad, map of system, logo, diesel freight and slogan "Ship It On The Frisco".................3.00

M&StL—scratch pad, logo and modern diesel freight locomotive 8.00

P RR—glass inkwell, metal cover, both marked "P RR" 30.00

P RR—glass postage stamp moistener, sponge insert, bottom marked "P RR"...............................20.00

SANTA FE—scratch pad, logo and blue line drawings of diesel on white....................................3.00

SOO LINE—metal scratch pad holder, 4″ x 8½″, logo and diesel train embossed on brass clip...................15.00*

SOO LINE—paper clip, 2¼″ x 2¾″, steel, logo and "SHIP TRAVEL" in red on gold......................10.00*

WABASH—scratch pad, flag logo and slogan "Those Who Know Ship And Go" also "Serving The Heart Of America" across bottom..3.50

STOCKS, CURRENCY AND BONDS

Railroad stock and bond certificates date back to the early days of the railroads, usually having the locomotive in their designs. Some of the engraving companies that did this work went out of business long ago. Many of these certificates feature a magnificent engine vignette and beautiful ornate scrollwork. There are collectors who specialize only in these. Some railroads issued their own currency, which was also a work of art. These interesting paper collectibles of years ago are in demand today.

STOCKS

B&O—100 shares, Common, Tom Thumb train vignette, brown border, issued 1903, cancelled 7.50

BO&SW—10 shares, Preferred, train and depot in small circle, green border, issued 1894, cancelled 9.50

CW&B—10 shares, Common, allegorical children, locomotive in center oval, 1880s, unissued 12.50

CB&Q—100 shares, Capital, locomotive vignette, brown border, issued 1895, cancelled 10.00

CGW—100 shares, Preferred, allegorical figures, train in center circle, rust border, issued 1965, cancelled 8.00

C&NW—100 shares, Common, winged mythological figures each side of railroad's herald in center, issued 1958, cancelled 5.00

CStPM&O—20 shares, Common, locomotive in center, brown border, issued 1922, cancelled 7.50

GM&N—100 shares, Common, trains in center oval, brown border, issued 1929, cancelled 6.00

GM&O—100 shares, Common, allegorical figures, train in center frame, blue border, issued 1941, cancelled 5.00

H&NH—5 shares, Capital, woodcut locomotive and ship, black border, issued 1846, cancelled, (rare) 30.00

M&StL—100 shares, Capital, allegorical female and locomotive vignette, purple border, early 1900s, unissued 10.00

Stock certificates

MK&T—10 shares, Capital, cattle vignette, violet border, issued 1887, cancelled 8.00

MK&T—100 shares, Common, locomotive and roundhouse vignette, green border, issued 1907, cancelled 6.00

CURRENCY

BRUNSWICK & ALBANY RR CO—$2.00, bank building obverse, train and depot vignette reverse, 1871 . . . . .25.00*

CENTRAL RAILROAD & BANKING CO OF GEORGIA—$2.00, cut of early train, 1861 . . . . .8.00

ERIE & KALAMAZOO RAILROAD BANK—$1.00, ships vignette in center, 1853 . . . . .25.00

ERIE & KALAMAZOO RAILROAD BANK—$10.00, vignette of people waving to passing train, 1854 . . . . .25.00*

MISSISSIPPI & ALABAMA RR CO—Figures and train in center vignette, portraits each corner, 1837 . . . . .30.00

MISSISSIPPI CENTRAL RR CO—25 cents, early passenger train, 1862 . . . . .5.00

MISSISSIPPI & TENNESSEE RR CO—5 cents, vignette Indians left side, American eagle center, 1862 . . . . .6.00

SOUTH CAROLINA RAILROAD CO—$2.00, early locomotive vignette in center, 1800s, uncirculated 5.00

WESTERN & ATLANTIC RR—50 cents, early train printed in red, 1862 . . . . .5.00

Early railroad currency

BONDS

HARTFORD, PROVIDENCE & FISHKILL RR CO.—$1,000
 bond, primitive train one end, embossed seal, issued 1854,
 redeemed 35.00
NORTHERN & SOUTHERN WEST VIRGINIA RR CO.—$1,000
 bond, eagle and train vignettes at top, all coupons intact at
 bottom, 1872 . . . . 45.00*
SOUTH MOUNTAIN RAILROAD CO.—$500.00 gold bond, train
 on bridge vignette, dated 1873, unissued, all coupons intact
 . . . . 37.50
TROY & GREENFIELD RR CO.—$1,000 bond, early train, dated
 1854, unissued, all coupons intact 57.50
UTAH & PLEASANT VALLEY RAILWAY CO.—$1,000 gold
 bond, miners, industry and train in center oval, issued 1878,
 partially redeemed 35.00

Early mortgage bond

TELEPHONES, TELEGRAPHY, INSULATORS

The most popular item with the collector of this category is the key and sounder. The telephone was also a part of the Station Agent's equipment, which included the scissors phone, candlestick desk phone, box-type wall phone, bell boxes, and miscellaneous related accessories. A lineman's portable phone with its case and shoulder strap is also included. All of this old depot telegraph and telephone equipment is collectible today. Prices vary depending on condition.

Glass insulators used on telegraph poles are also a part of this category, and the collecting of these has grown rapidly in the last decade. They were made in various colors, the most common being shades of green and blue. They are generally marked with the manufacturer's name, and many have patent dates. Those that are railroad-marked are of special interest ot the railroadiana collector. Value depends on condition and rarity.

TELEPHONES

DESK PHONE—candlestick type, 12″ tall, headset earpiece
 receiver, "American Tel. & Tel. Co., Pat. Jan. 14, 1913"
 . . . . 110.00*
DESK PHONE—dial in oval base, 5″ tall, headset mouthpiece
 and ear receiver, "Western Elec. Co.," ca. 1930-1940
 . . . . 75.00*
PORTABLE PHONE—lineman's, leather case with shoulder strap
 . . . . 95.00

SCISSORS PHONE—desk mount style, with hook and headset
 receiver, "Western Electric, Pat. 1915" 175.00
WALL PHONE—long box type, oak, 9½″ x 20½″, hook and
 headset receiver, "Push to Talk" button, "Western Electric"
 . . . . 185.00
WALL PHONE—oak box, 6½″ x 9″, with "Push to Talk, Release
 to Listen" button, hook and headset receiver, "W.E. Co."
 . . . . 100.00

BELL BOX—oak, 6½″ x 9″, railroad-marked, two bells on top, "Western Electric, type 295A".................45.00
DISPATCHERS TRANSMITTER HORN—with neck-strap and cord, "Western Electric"......................37.50
JACK-HOLE BOX—oak, 4½″ x 6¼″, three plugs, "W.E. Co." 25.00
PEG BOARD—wood panel, 18″ x 22″, ten position type with twenty pegs or plugs, marked "Western Elec. Co." .200.00
PEG BOARD—wood panel, 13″ x 9½″, four position type with nine pegs, marked "Bunnell W.U. Tel. Co.".....135.00

Depot phones · dial and candlestick type

TELEGRAPHY

Telegraph key, sounder, relay, code book

KEY—yellow brass base, oval, railroad-marked, "Chas. Cory & Sons, N.Y.".................................55.00*
KEY—Yellow brass base, oval, not RR-marked, "J.H. Bunnell & Co., N.Y."..................................37.50
KEY—Vibroplex, cast iron base, rectangular, brass maker's plate with serial number, side-swiper style key for high speed sending 85.00*

Vibroplex · telegraph speed key

RELAY—Cast iron base, rectangular, railroad-marked, "150 OHMS, J.H. Bunnell & Co., N.Y.".............55.00*
RESONATOR—Two adjustable cast iron arms, triangle-shaped wood box, "White Co., Worcester, Mass., Pat. Aug. 7, 1911" 135.00
RESONATOR—Three adjustable cast iron arms, triangle-shaped wood box, "White Co., Worcester, Mass., Pat. Aug. 7, 1911" 165.00*

Triple arm resonator with sounder

RESONATOR—Stationary, curved-back wood box mounted on iron pole 9″ tall, no maker's name.............35.00
RESONATOR—Stationary, model as above, complete with sounder...................................75.00
SOUNDER—Yellow brass, rectangle, mounted on wood base, railroad-marked, "J.H. Bunnell & Co., N.Y., Pat. May 7, 1895" 50.00*
SOUNDER—Yellow brass, rectangle, mounted on wood base, not railroad-marked, "J.H. Bunnell & Co., N.Y.," no pat. date 37.50
BOOK—*Manual of Railway Commercial And Wireless Telegraphy*, by Fred L. Meyer, Seventh Edition, 1914........30.00

BOOK—*Telegraphy Code, Mobile & Ohio RR*, issued St. Louis, May 10, 1920, soft cover......................25.00*

SIGN—Counter style, easel back, 5½″ x 9″, "Western Union Telegrams" on dark blue porcelainized metal......35.00

Glass insulator on pole mount

INSULATORS

B&O—aqua glass, "B&O" and "Pat. Jan. 25, 1870" raised on dome..25.00
B&O—white porcelain, "B&O" indented on base......15.00
CNR—white porcelain, "CNR" raised on dome.......18.00
CPR—light blue glass, raised letters around base......18.00*
CPR—light green glass, raised letters around base.....18.00
CPR—amethyst glass, raised letters around base......20.00
PRR—aqua green glass, raised initials on top of dome.15.00
PRR—dark green glass, raised initials on top of dome.17.50

TICKETS AND RELATED ITEMS

The railroads used a great variety of tickets down through the years. The colorful printed tickets in use before the turn of the century by roads long gone are in greater demand and bring high prices. Many collectors specialize in the small, card stock tickets from as many different railroads as possible. Also included are the small envelopes given travelers to protect their tickets. With the advent of the diesel, the earlier steam era envelopes were replaced by folder types having an inside pocket. Those featuring name trains are especially desirable. Every conductor had his own ticket punch, which had particular markings in the die, to perforate the tickets. The collector can accumulate any number of these old ticket punches, each with a different die mark. Ticket punches that are railroad-marked are priced higher.

Validators were used in the railroad's ticket offices to stamp the railroad's name, location, and date on the traveler's ticket, validating it. Those from the last century in good condition, complete with ribbon and die, have greater value. Spare dies for these machines can also be found, and they are priced according to the rarity of the railroad's name on them. Rubber stamps used in depots to imprint additional words in ink on the ticket, such as "First Class," "One Way Coach," name train, town name, etc., are now being picked up, too. Another item to look for in this category is the small cardboard seat check the conductor gave the passenger when he picked up the ticket. Those from before the turn of the century are hard to come by. Last but not least: Don't overlook the ticket cabinets with roll-down front used in small town depots years ago.

TICKETS

B&M—Commutation, five rides, card type, 1892.......5.00
BURLINGTON ROUTE—Commutation, ten rides, local, card type, 1900.................................3.00
C&NW—Emigrant passage, coupon strip with stub, paper, 1877 ....8.00

C&NW—1000 mile coupon booklet, partially used, 1886 ....12.00
CGW—1000 mile ticket booklet, unused, 1903.......15.00
CNS&M—Child's half-fare ticket, local, card stock, unissued 1.00

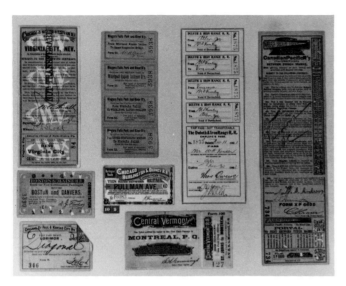

Miscellaneous tickets

CStP&KC—Half-fare ticket, local, paper stock, 1893....6.00
CV—Mileage ticket, 500 miles, folded type, cardboard, 1886
....8.00
ERR—Commutation, 60 rides, Allendale and New York, card type,
1921...2.50
FITCHBURG RR—One First Class passage, local, with stub, card-
board, 1880..5.00
GN—One First Class passage, local, card stock, 1922...2.00
GN—First Class half-fare permit, St. Paul to Duluth, paper, 1900
....3.50
MP—Excursion ticket, Leavenworth—Kansas City, paper, 1902
....2.00
MP—Carbonized ticket booklet, paper stock, unused, 1960
....3.00
MONON—Carbonized ticket booklet, paper stock, unused, 1960s
....3.00

NYC&StL—One First Class passage, local, card stock, 1886
....4.50
NYNH&H—One passage half-fare, local, card stock, 1890
....3.50
NYLE&W—One First Class passage, local, card stock, 1893
....2.25
NP—One First Class passage, local, card stock, 1891...2.50
NP—25 ride individual commutation ticket book, local, unissued,
1920s...6.00
PRR—Coach ticket, local, card stock, 1926...........2.00
ROCK ISLAND—One way coach reservation ticket on the Rocket,
card stock, 1942..1.50
SOO LINE—Six-month round-trip coach ticket with stub, paper
stock, 1952..2.00
SOO LINE—Banana messenger's ticket book, coupons for 10
trips, partially used, 1930s, scarce...............25.00*
W&StP—First Class, local, card stock, unused, 1879...8.00

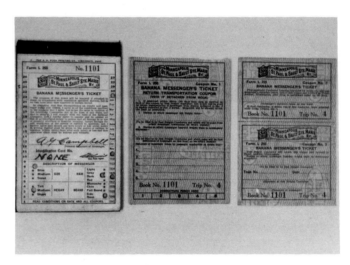

Banana messenger's ticket book

TICKET ENVELOPES

B&O—Train at depot frontside, system map/logo back, blue-white
envelope, 1940s...............................4.00
C&O—Chessie kitten frontside, map/logo back, green-white
envelope, 1940s...............................4.00
CMStP&P—Logo and electric train frontside, Gallatin Gateway
Yellowstone Park scene back, 1930s...............8.00*
GN—Logo/Empire Builder front and back, blue-white folder,
1960s...2.00
IC—5 name diesel trains frontside, system map/logo back, white-
rust envelope, 1950s..........................3.00
MILWAUKEE ROAD—Views of Superdome Hiawatha and logos
both sides, yellow envelope, 1950s...............2.00
MO-PAC—Eagle diesel streamliner frontside, logo/flying Eagle
back, red/black envelope, 1950s..................4.00
NP—Logo and Old Faithful geyser frontside, logo and Great Falls
Yellowstone Park scene back, 1930s..............8.00*

Steam-era ticket envelopes

NP—Dome cars under semaphore signals frontside, logo back, red folder, 1960s..............................2.00

NYC—Old State House, Boston, frontside, logo back, green-white envelope, 1960s................................2.00

ROCK ISLAND—Logo/Rocket frontside, logo/map back, red envelope, 1960s................................2.00

SOO LINE—Entitled "Trains Of Steel" and logo frontside, logo and dining car scene back, 1930s...............10.00*

TICKET PUNCHES

B&M—Fleur-de-lis punch mark, "Pat. July 18, 1882"..25.00*
CGW—"L" punch mark.........................30.00
CNW—"½" punch mark........................20.00
GN—"2d" punch mark.........................25.00
NYC—"B" punch mark.........................20.00
PRR—"L" punch mark, "Pat. Dec. 23, 1884".......30.00
Unmarked—heart punch mark.....................6.00
Unmarked—clover punch mark...................6.00*
Unmarked—crescent punch mark.................6.00
Unmarked—star punch mark.....................6.00
Unmarked—dual marking, star and shoe...........10.00
Unmarked—satellite punch mark and edge cutter pattern
....12.00

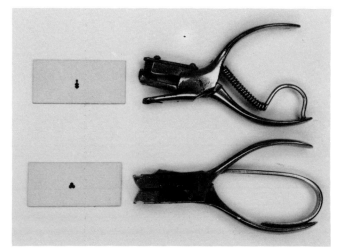

Conductor's ticket punches

TICKET DATER VALIDATING MACHINES

HILL'S MODEL A—Centennial dater, complete with die and ribbon. "Great Northern Railway, Anoka, Minn." Dates 1946-1957 ....135.00

HILL'S MODEL A-D—Centennial dater, complete with die and ribbon, "Nor. Pac. Ry. Little Falls, Minn." Dates 1952-1963
....125.00

COSMO MODEL NO.2—Complete with die and ribbon. "C.R.I. & P Ry. Lewis, Ia." Dates 1910-1959............75.00

COSMO MODEL NO.3—Complete with die and ribbon. "Erie R.R. Co. Decatur, Ind." Dates 1910-1969........85.00

Ticket validators and dies

SPARE TICKET DATER DIES

"CMStP&P RR, Glenview, Ill."....................45.00
"CMStP RY, SOO LINE, CRI&P RY, Mpls. Depot" (triple marked)
....75.00
"CRI&P RY, Hope, Minn."......................45.00

"GN RY, Pekin, N.D."..........................55.00
"IC RR. 9279, Albany, La.".......................35.00
"MO PAC RR CO—Prescott, Ark."................40.00
"NO.PAC.RY—Ritzville, Wash."..................50.00

Ticket cabinet - roll-down front type

TICKET CABINETS

Oak, slanted roll front, large size, 36″ high, Pool Bros. Mfgrs.
. . . . 275.00*
Oak, vertical roll front, small size, 8″ x 15″ x 28″, National Ticket
Case Co. 200.00

RUBBER HAND STAMPS

"ONE WAY COACH"—Black upright handle atop rectangular
rubber die base. 5.00
"ONE WAY FIRST CLASS"—Black upright handle atop rec-
tangular rubber die base. 4.50
"EMPIRE BUILDER"—Name train, one piece finger-molded nar-
row rubber die. 2.50
"LACROSSE"—Town name, one piece finger-molded narrow rub-
ber die. 1.75
"ROOMETTE"—One piece finger-molded narrow rubber die
. . . . .2.00

Miscellaneous rubber stamps

SEAT CHECKS

BCR&M—1870s, blue card stock. 8.00
C&NW, Dakota Division—1870s, lavender card stock. . .4.00*
M&StP, River Division—1870s, yellow card stock. 6.00*
NY&E—1870s, orange card stock, cut of train. 5.00*
NYNH&H—1870s, green card stock, cut of train. 5.00*
W&StP—1870s, green card stock. 8.00

Early card stock seat checks

TIMETABLES

Many collectors price public timetables on a yearly scale, starting with a base price for the most recent date and increasing each previous year to 1900 by a nominal amount, making exceptions for the uncommon. The colorful timetables previous to the 1940s picturing trains, legendary figures, ornate logos, and interesting slogans on their covers, generally bring the higher prices, as do those from short lines, narrow gauge and defunct roads. The early fold-out pictorial timetables from the last half of the nineteenth century are highly prized and have accelerated substantially in price. Many of these were a large single sheet with a colored map on one side, with illustrations, advertising and train schedules on the other side, folding into a pamphlet. The earliest timetables, such as the small card or single sheet of paper listing train schedules, are the rarities.

Employee timetables also evolved from a single sheet to booklet and folder types. They were issued for employees only, containing restricted information as to the operation of the trains, and were never distributed to the general public. Those from early now defunct roads have a higher value. Some collectors specialize in employee timetables only.

PUBLIC

Public timetables - steam and diesel era

Miscellaneous pictorial folding timetables, pre-1900

ALTON RAILROAD—1932, May 29, engineer and fireman in cab on cover 12.00
AMTRAK—1972, Jan.16 . . . . .3.00
AT&SF—1882, Dec. 21, pictorial fold-out 85.00
ACL—1951, Sept. 30 . . . . .4.00
B&A—1903, Jan. 12, South Station on cover, local . . .10.00
B&M—1879, June 30, Summer Arrangement, folder . . .25.00
B&M—1910, June 20, local 8.50
B&M—1928, Oct. 29, Minute Man on cover 6.00
B&O—1884, June 15, pictorial fold-out 65.00
B&O—1936, April 26 . . . . .5.50
B&OSW—1911, No.1 . . . . .10.00
BN—1970, Oct. 25 . . . . .1.50
BIG FOUR ROUTE—1936, June 1, Cincinnati Union Terminal on cover 6.50
BURLINGTON ROUTE—1930, July-August 7.50
C&A—1882, Feb., pictorial fold-out 70.00
C&EI—1948, Dec. 12, Georgia streamliner on cover 6.00
C&NW—1882, Nov. 12, pictorial fold-out 75.00
C&NW—1900, Dec. 9, passenger train on cover 35.00

C&NW—1939, April 30, "400" and streamliners on cover 6.00
C&O—1909, May 23 . . . . .15.00
CB&Q—1878, Feb-June, pictorial fold-out 75.00
CGW—1912, Mar. 1, Corn Belt emblem on cover 20.00
CM&StP—1897, Aug. 1, dining car interior on cover, pictorial fold-out 65.00
CMStP&P—1937, June-July 5.00
CPR—1913, Feb. 1, beaver and shield on cover 15.00
CV—1913, July 1 . . . . .12.50
COLORADO MIDLAND—1909, July 25.00
CStP&KC—1889, July 28, maple leaf emblem on cover (scarce) 45.00
D&H—1907, Summer, train at night on cover 12.50
D&RG—1893, Sept., pictorial fold-out 55.00
D&RGW—1951, June 1, Royal Gorge on cover 6.00
DM&N—1912, July, No. 39 . . . . .17.50
DSS&A—1940, Dec. 15 . . . . .12.50
ERIE—1906, June 24 . . . . .15.00
FEC—1951, Sept. 30, diesel on cover 3.50

FITCHBURG RAILROAD—1884, Dec., pictorial fold-out (rare)
....80.00
FRISCO SYSTEM—1903, February...............10.00
GM&O—1947, December.........................4.00
GN—1901, July 15, Cascade tunnel on cover.........35.00
GN—1916, May 14, local.......................15.00
GN—1930, June, mountain goat logo on cover.......8.00
GN—1948, Oct-Nov-Dec., streamliners on cover.......4.00
GTP—1915, June 6.............................8.50
HARLEM EXTENSION RR—1871, May 29, single sheet, wood-cut of primitive train (rare)...................95.00*

Framed single sheet timetable

IC—1899, April 20, Southern Fast Mail emblem on cover
....22.50
IR—1938, Sept. 6, electric train on cover...........6.00
IRON MOUNTAIN ROUTE—1885, Oct. 20, pictorial fold-out
....75.00
JCRR—1944, March 12.........................4.00
KCS—1947, June 22, "Southern Belle" streamliner on cover
....4.00
LACKAWANNA RAILROAD—1901, Sept. 1........12.00
LACKAWANNA RAILROAD—1952, Sept. 28, "Phoebe Snow" streamliner on cover.........................3.50
L&N—1944, Dec. 17............................4.00
LS&MS—1857, Mar. 31, card type, 3″ x 5″ (rare)....50.00
LS&MS—1878, May 12, pictorial fold-out...........95.00

LS&MS—1901, Jan., Fast Mail sack on cover........35.00
LV—1905, May 14.............................15.00
MEC—1899, May 1, pictorial fold-out..............45.00
MEX.NAT.RR—1897, Sept. 9....................20.00
M&O—1914, Nov. 22..........................8.00
M&StL—1907, June 2, "Albert Lea Route" logo on cover
....30.00
MKT—1901, Jan., figure of "Katy" on cover........25.00
MP—1946, Nov. 24, "Eagles" streamliner on cover.....5.00
MONON ROUTE—1946, Nov. 17.................4.00
NAT. RYS. MEX—1929, Oct-Nov.................8.50
NEW HAVEN RAILROAD—1967, April 30..........3.00
NICKEL PLATE—1893, May 28, pictorial fold-out....45.00
N&W—1953, June 7............................4.00
NP—1880, Sept. (rare).........................125.00
NP—1887, July, pictorial fold-out................75.00
NP—1929, Feb-Mar...........................6.00
NYC—1931, Sept 27, passenger train on cover.......6.00
NYC&HR—1884, Nov. 11, pictorial fold-out..........65.00
NY&NH RR—1855, card type, 3″ x 5″, (rare).......50.00
NC&StL—1947, Spring.........................4.00
P&R—1903, Nov. 29, P & R emblem, fold-out.......15.00
PC—1971, March 3............................1.50
PM—1946, Aug. 10, "Pere Marquette" streamliner on cover
....5.00
PRR—1887, March 23, pictorial fold-out...........75.00
PRR—1945, Sept. 30, turntable on cover.............8.00
PRR—1963, Feb. 10...........................3.00
READING RAILWAY SYSTEM—1947, Sept. 28.......4.00
ROCK ISLAND—1924, June 22...................6.00
RUT—1913, June 22...........................13.00
SEABOARD RAILWAY—1945, Jan. 15.............4.00
SL&SW—1947, Dec. 21.........................4.00
StP&D—1899, Spring, pictorial fold-out (rare).......85.00
StPM&M—1886, July, pictorial fold-out (rare)......100.00
SOO LINE—1905, Aug. 1, local..................25.00
SOO LINE—1915, March 17.....................20.00
SOO LINE—1963, Dec. 10......................6.00
SP—1912, Dec., Sunset Ogden & Shasta Route logo on cover
....15.00
SP—1970, Oct. 20............................2.00
SP&S—1957, Jan. 1...........................8.00
SR—1951, Aug. 5, "Crescent" & "Southerner" streamliners on cover...................................4.00
STONINGTON LINE BOAT AND RAIL—1880, Summer, pictorial fold-out (rare)........................85.00
T&P—1926, April 15..........................6.00
UP—1901, Oct. 1.............................15.00
UP—1922, Nov. 15...........................8.00
UP—1953, March 1, steam & diesel trains on cover...4.00*
WAB—1906, February, Niagara Falls on cover.......15.00
WAB—1926, Jan-Feb., steam train on cover.........8.00
WAB—1945, Nov. 18..........................5.00
WC—1900, Feb..............................25.00
WP—1951, April 29...........................4.00
W&LE—1894, Feb. 15, pictorial fold-out...........55.00

EMPLOYEE TIMETABLES

C&NW—Wisconsin Division, No. 441, April 30, 1950...5.00
CRI&P—Des Moines Division, No. 4, Oct. 31, 1965....4.00
CStPM&O—Western Division, No. 2, Oct. 30, 1955....6.00
GN—Willmar Division, No. 124, Oct. 30, 1966.......5.00
IC—Iowa Division, No. 26, April 26, 1959...........4.50*
MKT—N. Texas Division, No. 28, Jan. 8, 1956.......5.00
MStP&SSM—Twin City Terminal Division, No. 9, July 12, 1931
....8.00*
NP—Dakota Division, No. 20, July 6, 1902.........12.50*
NP—Idaho Division, No. 36, Jan. 1, 1912...........8.00
W&StP—No. 113, Nov. 25, 1883.................30.00*
WILLIAMSPORT & ELMIRA RR—No. 4, May 25, 1857 (rare)
....50.00
WP&YR—No. 92, June 16, 1946.................10.00

Employee timetables

TOOLS, STEAM ERA VINTAGE

Collecting old railroad-marked tools from the steam era used by workers in the roundhouses, shops, depots, and for track maintenance has become a hobby for many. Some specialize in the small hand-tools only, while others collect all types, both large and small. The railroad marking is found somewhere on the metal or on the wood handle.

Miscellany of railroad-marked tools

"AT&SF RY"—Cold steel chisel, 8″ long............8.00
"B&M RR"—Ax, "TRUE TEMPER," 30″ handle.....37.50
"C&NW"—Monkey wrench, all metal, size 18, "TRIMO," 16″ long
....15.00
"C&NW"—Double-headed open end curved wrench, 10″ long
....10.00
"CB&Q"—Track shovel, "HUSKEY"................25.00

"CB&Q"—Steel rail splitter, V shape, "ONA," head 8″ long
....8.00
"CGW"—Auger bit w/wood head and handle, No. 1001,
    "MILLERS FALLS", 14″.....................22.00*
"CGW"—Screwdriver, rivetted wood handle, 7″........6.50*
"CM&StP RY"—Monkey wrench, all metal, "INTERMEDIATE,"
    12″ long...................................15.00
"CMStP&P"—Cold steel chisel, 8″ long.............6.00
"CMStP&P RR"—Ball pein hammer, "FAIRMOUNT," 14″ handle
....12.00
"CMStP&P RR"—Track pick, "BEAVER FALLS," 36″ handle
....25.00
"CStPM&O RY"—Track adz, "BEAVER FALLS," 34″ handle
....22.50
"CStPM&O RY"—Single-headed open-end curved wrench, 7″
    long......................................10.00
"CStPM&O RY"—Double-headed open-end curved wrench, 13″
    long......................................14.00
"DSS&A RY"—Spiking maul, "SLUG DEVIL," 34½″ handle
....30.00
"GN"—Monkey wrench, all metal, size 12, "TRIMO," 11″ long
....15.00
"GN RY"—Hatchet, depot type, "TRUE TEMPER," 13½″ handle
....37.50*

"GN RY"—Ball pein hammer, "TRUE TEMPER," 16" handle 12.50
"GN RY"—Cold steel chisel, 7½" long 8.00
"GN RY CO."—Track shovel, "AMES HUSKEY," 38" long with handle 22.50
"IC"—Track adz, "ALDUSHT, CHGO.," 34" handle . . . 15.00
"LS&MS"—Double-headed open-end curved wrench, 12" long 20.00
"M&StL"—Hatchet, depot type, claw nail-puller head, 15" handle 45.00
"M&StL"—Double-faced sledge, 35" handle 30.00
"M&StL"—Cold steel chisel, 9" long 8.00
"MT RY"—Pliers, "DROP FORGED," 6½" 7.50*
"NYC RR"—Cold steel chisel, 6½" long 4.00
"NYC&HR"—Double-headed open-end curved wrench, 12" long 25.00
"NPR"—Monkey wrench, wood handle, "BILLINGS," 12½" long 15.00
"NPR"—Monkey wrench, wood handle, "B & Co.," 15" long 16.00
"NPR"—Ball pein hammer, "TRUE TEMPER," 16" handle 12.50
"NP RR"—Coal shovel, "AMES RED EDGE," 42½" long with handle 25.00
"NP RR"—Hand saw, "E.C. ATKINS," wood handle, 26" long 22.50*
"NOR.PAC."—Steel chisel for gouging wood, 12½" 1 5.00
"OMAHA RY."—Monkey wrench, wood handle, "Pat. 1901, H.D. Smith," 8½" long 20.00
"RY.EX. AGY."—Hatchet, depot type, "PLUMB" 14" handle 42.00

Double-end wrenches

"RY.EX.AGY."—Crate opener, steel, hammer head and nail-puller, "DIAMOND," 9" 15.00*
"R.I. LINES"—Coal shovel, coal-stove type, cast iron, 16" long 32.50
"R.I. LINES"—Tie tongs, "ALDUSHT CO. CHGO.", 29" long 26.00
"ROCK ISLAND"—Double-headed open-end curved wrench, 11½" long 10.00
"St.P.CY.RY."—Steel lining bar, 58½" long 18.00
"SOO LINE"—Spiking maul, "SLUG DEVIL," 34½" handle 30.00
"SOO LINE"—Cold steel chisel, 8½" long 8.00
"UNION PACIFIC"—Tool box, wood, iron handle, 28" long 17.50
"UNION PACIFIC"—Monkey wrench, all metal, "W&B RR SPECIAL," 8" long 12.50

TOURIST GUIDES AND BROCHURES

Railroad guidebooks were published as early as the 1850s. Many were beautifully illustrated with colored maps, train schedules, and interesting advertisements. Most of these were privately published. Many of the early guidebooks have a very high value placed on them. Those published by the railroads are especially desirable.

Thousands of travel brochures were distributed by the railroads down through the years encouraging the tourists to ride their trains. Many were discarded after the trip ended, making them scarce today. Those from the early 1900s are the most colorful and interesting. Copies in fine condition bring good prices.

Among the numerous soft-cover books promoting tourist travel were the string-tied scenic guidebooks containing large colored pictures of scenery along the railroad's route. These were in vogue in the early 1900s, and today collectors are seeking them out.

The railroads issued colorful brochures to lure the settlers, telling them of the many farming advantages on the lands available along their right-of-ways. Many collectors specialize in these.

GUIDE BOOKS (Hard cover)

APPLETON'S—*Northern and Eastern Traveler's Guide,* 1853
.... 65.00*
CROFUTT'S—*Trans-Continental Tourists' Guide,* 1871.50.00
HARPER'S—*New York and Erie Rail-Road Guide Book,* 1852
.... 75.00*
HITTEL'S—*Hand Book of Pacific Coast Travel,* 1885..35.00
NELSON'S—*Pictorial Guide Book, Union Pacific Railroad,* 1871
.... 30.00
NELSON'S—*Pictorial Guide Book, Central Pacific Railroad,* 1871
.... 30.00
Railroad *Tourist Guide,* 1879..................... 35.00
The Official Northern Pacific R.R. Guide, 1893....... 55.00
William's *Pacific Tourist & Guide Across the Continent,* 1879
.... 50.00

Early guide books

TRAVEL BROCHURES

B&O—*Reasons Why,* booklet, 1901................. 8.50
B&O—"Eastern Summer Trips," folder, 1931........ 5.50
BURLINGTON ROUTE—*Heritage From the Gods,* booklet, 1936
.... 3.00
BURLINGTON ROUTE—"Mississippi River Scenic Line," folder,
6-15-54................................... 3.50*
CENTRAL IOWA RY—*The Great Northwest,,* booklet, 1887
(rare) 35.00
C&NW—"Century of Progress," 1934, folder.......... 3.50
CM&StP—"Hunting in the Cascades," folder, 1920s.... 5.00
CMStP&P—*The Trail Of The Olympian,* booklet, 1930..6.50
CMRY—*Early Days,* hard cover book with 12 litho. scenes along
the route traversed by the C M Ry., 1902 (rare)...150.00
CP—"Canadian Rocky Mountain Resorts," folder, 1911
.... 8.50*
D&H—"The Adirondacks, Our Great National Playground,"
folder, 1920s............................... 7.50
D&RG—"Panaramic Views along the Scenic Line of the World,"
folder, 1893............................... 20.00
FEC—*East Coast of Florida,* booklet, 1900.......... 15.00
GN—*Seven Sunsets,* booklet, 1915................. 12.50
GN—*The Oriental Limited,* booklet, 1914........... 15.00
GN—*The New Oriental Limited,* booklet, 1924....... 10.00
GN—"Glacier National Park, Hotels & Tours", folder, 1915
.... 7.50
LV—*In 3 States,* booklet, 1880s (rare).............. 35.00
MIDLAND ROUTE—*Thru the Rockies of Colorado,* booklet,
1910 .... 20.00
NP—*Along the Scenic Highway,* booklet, 1914....... 12.50*
NP—*6000 Miles through Wonderland,* booklet, 1893..25.00
NYC—"Hudson River," folder, 1934................. 5.50
PRR—"Eastern Tours Summer 1929," folder.......... 4.50

Tourist brochures

ROCK ISLAND SYSTEM—"Across the Continent in a Tourist
Sleeping Car," folder, 1903..................... 15.00
ROCK ISLAND—*California,* booklet, 1912........... 10.00
SANTA FE—*The California Limited,* booklet, 1914-1915
.... 7.50
SANTA FE—*Along Your Way,* booklet, 1949......... 3.00
SOO LINE—*By Way of the Canyons,* booklet, 1907...12.50
SOO LINE—"See Europe if you Will but see America First,"
folder, 1907............................... 10.00
SP&S—"The Scenic Columbia River," folder.......... 7.50
UP—*A Glimpse of the Great Salt Lake,* booklet, 1894, (rare)
.... 30.00
UP—*Summer Tours,* booklet, 1933................. 3.50
UP—*California Calls You,* booklet, 1922............. 8.00*

STRING-TIED SCENIC GUIDE BOOKS

CM&StP—*Lake Michigan to Puget Sound,* 1924......18.00*
D&RG—*Rocky Mountain Views,* 1917...............20.00
D&RG—*Heart of the Rockies,* 1910...............25.00
M&PP—*The Pike's Peak Region,* 1922.............15.00
SANTA FE—*The Great Southwest,* (Fred Harvey) 1914
....35.00
SP—*The Shasta Route,* 1916....................18.00*
SP—*The Overland Trail,* 1923..................15.00
WP—*From Salt Lake City ot San Francisco Bay,* 1915
....20.00*

String-tied scenic guide books

SETTLER'S ADVERTISING BROCHURES

BURLINGTON ROUTE—"Home Seeker's Excursions to the
  West, Northwest and Southwest," folder, 1908.....10.00*
CM&StP—"Three Forks Country, Montana," folder, 1913
....12.00
CM&StP—"Montana, The Treasure State," folder, 1915
....10.00*
CM&StP—*The Granary of the Northwest,* booklet, 1916
....8.00
GN—*Zone Of Plenty,* booklet, 1929................6.00
M&O—"Lands in Alabama and Mississippi," folder, 1901
....12.50*
NP—*North Dakota Farms for the Settler,* 64 page booklet, 1916
....8.00
SP—*California for the Settler,* booklet, 1922.........8.00

Settler's brochures

TOY TRAINS

Collecting old toy trains is one of today's most popular hobbies, and an ever increasing number of railroadiana collectors are being attracted to them. Down through the years, millions of these toy trains were made out of wood, tin, and cast iron, in pull-type, friction, wind-up, live steam, and electric. Many collectors specialize in the cast iron sets, while others collect the early wind-ups or electric models, but most generalize. Names most sought after are Ives, American Flyer, and Lionel. Condition is a very important factor in pricing. An early set in its original box in fine condition commands a very high price. Reproductions are being made.

WOOD—Pull type, set, locomotive/tender, two passenger cars,
  lithographed designs on paper glued to sides, ca. 1870
....300.00
TIN—Pull type, set, locomotive, 3 passenger cars, original paint,
  22″ length, ca. 1870s......................200.00
CAST IRON—Pull type, set, locomotive, tender, 2 freight cars,
  nickel finish, 21″ length, "Pat. June 8, 1880, Carpenter"
....325.00

CAST IRON—4-4-0 type, locomotive with tender, original black
  finish, 21″ long, ca. 1880s. "Wilkins"...........275.00
CAST IRON—Set, #999 locomotive, tender, 2 cattle cars, caboose
  original paint, marked "M.C.R.R.", ca. 1890s.....250.00
CAST IRON—#1101 locomotive, tender, 2 passenger cars, nickel
  finish, marked "C.R.I. & P.R.R." ca. 1890s, "Wilkins"
....325.00

CAST IRON—Set, #857 locomotive, tender, 4 passenger cars, "Washington," "Narcissus," red/gold decor, "Pennsylvania R.R. Co., 1927, Hubley".....................300.00

CAST IRON—2-2-0 type "Big 6" locomotive w/tender, orig. finish, ca. 1890s................................175.00*

Cast iron Big 6 locomotive

LIVE STEAM—Set, locomotive, tender, baggage & 2 passenger cars, original paint, "VULCAN" Germany, ca. 1890s 500.00

WOOD/TIN—Friction type, locomotive only, original red/gold trim decor, ca. 1900s............................125.00

WIND-UP—"American Flyer," tinplate, 0 gauge set, locomotive, tender, 3 passenger cars, original box, ca. 1910...200.00*

WIND-UP—"Hafner's" tinplate, 0 gauge set, locomotive, tender, 3 passenger cars, "Overland Flyer," original red and yellow decor, ca. 1930s.............................125.00

ELECTRIC—Ives, 0 gauge set, electric type locomotive #3200, 2 passenger cars, litho "The Ives Railway Lines," ca. 1911 ....200.00

ELECTRIC—Ives, 0 gauge set, #1117 engine, tender, 3 passenger cars, litho "Limited Vestibule Express," ca. 1920s.275.00

ELECTRIC—Lionel, standard gauge set, #318E engine, 3 passenger cars, ca. 1930s....................1,500.00

ELECTRIC—Lionel, 0 gauge set, #258 engine, tender, 3 passenger cars, original box, ca. 1930...........325.00

ELECTRIC—Lionel, 0 gauge set, #1666 engine, tender, gondola car, box car, milk car, caboose, original cartons, ca. 1950s 150.00

Tin wind-up train

WATCHES, WATCH FOBS AND EMBLEM CHARMS

American watchmakers were required to meet certain rigid standards established by the railroads, including inspection and servicing routinely performed by qualified jewelers. It would be wise for the collector, not knowledgeable of authentic railroad pocket watches, to make a thorough study in this field before investing in them. The fact that a watch may have a train engraving on the case, for instance, does not necessarily mean that the movement is an approved railroad grade. Watches not in running order, or having dial cracks, or cases badly worn or dented, must be discounted. All watches listed here are in perfect condition.

Thousands of Brotherhood and railroad emblem charms were made to be worn on a gold watch chain across the vest. Also, fobs were made to be hung on a leather or woven wire mesh strap or black satin ribbon from the pants watch pocket. These authentic old emblem charms and watch fobs are high on the list and command very good prices. There are current reproduction railroad watch fobs (leather strap type) on the market, and these should not be confused with the old.

KEY TO ABBREVIATIONS

ADJ—movement has been adjusted to railroad specifications.

17J—number of jewels in the movement, 21J, 23J, etc..

5P—adjusted position of movement, as 5 positions, 6 positions, etc..

992—numbers denote model of movement and railroad grade.

16S—size of watch movement and case, 18 size large, 16 size smaller.

REG—regular standard arabic numeral dial.

MONT—Montgomery minute marginal numeral dial.

YGF—yellow gold filled case.

WGF—white gold filled case.

BALL—(Elgin) *333, 17J, 5P, 18S, REG,* silveroid case
. . . . 275.00
BALL—(Hamilton) *17J, ADJ, 18S, REG,* silveroid case
. . . . 200.00
BALL—(Hamilton) *999, 17J, 5P, 18S, REG,* silver case, train
engraving 300.00
BALL—(Waltham) *17J, 5P, 16S, REG, YGF* case. . . .180.00
BALL—(Illinois) *19J, 5P, 16S, REG, YGF* case 200.00
BALL—(Hamilton) *999, 21J, 5P, 18S,* sterling case, gold inlaid
locomotive 425.00
BALL—(Hamilton) *999B, 21J, 6P, 16S, MONT, YGF* case
. . . . 325.00
BALL—(Hamilton) *21J, 5P, 16S, REG, WGF* case. . .245.00
BALL—(Hamilton) *23J, 5P, 16S, REG, YGF* case. . . .600.00
BALL—(Swiss) *21J, 6P, 16S, REG, YGF* case 275.00
ELGIN—*17J, ADJ, 18S,* key wind, Roman numeral dial, YGF hunting case, locomotive engraving. 200.00
ELGIN—B.W. Raymond, *19J, 5P, 18S,* up & down indicator dial,
YGF case 750.00
ELGIN—B.W. Raymond, *21J, 5P, 16S, REG, YGF* case
. . . . 175.00
ELGIN—Father Time, *21J, 5P, 16S, MONT, YGF* case
. . . . 165.00
ELGIN—*379, 21J, 5P, 18S, REG, YGF* case. 160.00
ELGIN—Veritas, *21J, 5P, 16S, REG, YGF* case. 185.00
ELGIN—Veritas, *23J, ADJ, 18S, REG, YGF* case, locomotive
engraving 285.00
ELGIN—Veritas, *23J, 5P, 18S, REG, YGF* case. 325.00
HAMILTON—*17J, ADJ, 18S,* Roman numeral dial, *YGF* hunting
case, train engraving. .200.00
HAMILTON—*996, 19J, 5P, 16S, REG, YGF* case. . . .275.00
HAMILTON—*940, 21J, 5P, 18S, MONT, YGF* case. .150.00
HAMILTON—*992, 21J, 5P, 16S, MONT, YGF* case. .150.00
HAMILTON—*992B, 21J, 6P, 16S, REG, YGF* case. . .200.00
HAMILTON—*950, 23J, 5P, 16S,* dial marked "23 Jewels-Railway
Special," *YGF* case. 425.00
HAMILTON—*950B, 23J, 6P, 16S* dial marked "23 Jewels-Railway
Special," *YGF* case. 450.00
HAMPDEN—New Railway, *21J, 5P, REG, WGF* case.175.00
HAMPDEN—*17J,* Special Adjusted, *18S,* Roman numeral dial,
YGF hunting case, locomotive engraving. 250.00
HAMPDEN—Railway Special, *21J, ADJ, 18S, REG,* sterling case,
gold inlay locomotive. 250.00
HAMPDEN—Special Railway, *21J, 5P, 18S, REG, YGF* case
. . . . 225.00
HAMPDEN—Special Railway, *23J, 5P, 18S, REG, YGF* case
. . . . 350.00
HOWARD—Railroad Chronometer Series 10, *21J, 5P, 16S, REG,*
YGF case. 275.00
HOWARD—Railroad Chronometer Series 11, *21J, 5P, 16S,*
MONT, YGF case. 285.00
ILLINOIS—Abe Lincoln, *21J, 5P, 16S,* Ferguson dial, *YGF* case
. . . . 300.00*
ILLINOIS—Bunn Special, *21J, 6P, 16S, REG, YGF* case,
locomotive engraving. 225.00
ILLINOIS—Bunn Special, 60 Hour, *21J, 6P, 16S, REG, YGF* case
. . . . 285.00

Uncommon dial - Ferguson Patented

ILLINOIS—Burlington Special, *21J, ADJ, 16S, MONT, YGF* case
. . . . 185.00
ILLINOIS—Sangamo Special, *21J, 6P, 16S, REG, YGF* case
. . . . 250.00
ILLINOIS—Sangamo Special, *23J, 6P, 16S, MONT, YGF* case
. . . . 425.00*
ILLINOIS—Santa Fe Special, *21J, ADJ, 16S, MONT, YGF* case,
train engraving. 215.00
ROCKFORD—545, *21J, 5P, 16S, REG, YGF* case. . .175.00
ROCKFORD—505, *21J, 5P, 16S, REG, YGF* case. . .195.00
ROCKFORD—918, *21J, 5P, 18S, MONT,* sterling case,
locomotive engraving. 275.00*

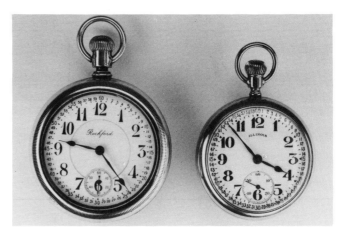

18 size and 16 size watches

SOUTH BEND—227, *21J, 5P, 16S, MONT, YGF* case
. . . . 175.00
SOUTH BEND—295 *21J, 5P, 16S, MONT, YGF* case
. . . . 195.00
WALTHAM—Riverside, *19J, 5P, 16S, MONT, YGF* case
. . . . 195.00
WALTHAM—Vanguard, *19J, 5P, 16S,* Canadian dial, *YGF* case
. . . . 185.00

WALTHAM—Crescent Street, *21J, 5P, 16S, MONT, YGF* case 195.00
WALTHAM—645, *21J, 5P, 16S, REG, YGF* case 275.00
WALTHAM—845, *21J, 5P, 18S, REG, YGF* case 150.00
WALTHAM—Vanguard, *21J, ADJ, 18S*, Canadian dial, silveroid case, locomotive engraving 200.00

WALTHAM—Maximum, *23J, ADJ, 16S, REG*, 18K gold case 950.00
WALTHAM—Vanguard, *23J, 6P, 16S, REG, YGF* case 295.00
WALTHAM—Vanguard, *23J, 6P, 16S*, Up & Down indicator dial, YGF case 750.00

WATCH FOBS AND EMBLEM CHARMS

"DAVENPORT LOCOMOTIVE WORKS, DAVENPORT, IOWA"—Oval, silver plated copper, locomotive in center, leather strap type 95.00*
"INT'L. ASSN. OF RWY. SPECIAL AGENTS AND POLICE"—round, bronze, train encircled by "Safety First" on blue enamel, leather strap type 75.00*
"RAILWAY SIGNAL ASSOCIATION"—round, brass, train and semaphores in center, leather strap type 55.00
"STANLEY MERRILL & PHILLIPS RY. CO., STANLEY, WISC."—oval, bronze, locomotive center, "1909" above, "Spur 5" below, leather strap type 100.00*

Leather strap watch fobs

"LADIES AUXILLARY O.R.C. MEMPHIS 1907"—ornate bronze fob, leather strap type 65.00
"NORTHERN PACIFIC"—monad logo, enamel on gold, black satin ribbon type 85.00

"ASSOC. SOCIETY OF LOCOMOTIVE ENGINEERS & FIREMEN"—ornate gold/enamel emblem, black satin ribbon type 95.00
"BROTHERHOOD OF RAILWAY TRAINMEN"—ornate gold/enamel BRT emblem, woven wire mesh type . . . 50.00
"BROTHERHOOD OF LOCOMOTIVE FIREMEN AND ENGINEERS"—ornate gold/enamel emblem, vest chain type 45.00*
"BROTHERHOOD OF RAILROAD TRAINMEN"—maltese cross type, gold/black enamel, BRT insignia at center, vest chain emblem charm 45.00
"KANSAS CITY SOUTHERN"—bronze disc 1″ diameter, "Golden Spike Anniversary, 1897-1947," vest chain fob 20.00
"NORTHERN PACIFIC"—inlay enamel monad logo on gold filled disc, 1⅛″ diameter, vest chain emblem charm 50.00

Watch with chain and emblem charm

WAX SEALERS AND ACCESSORIES

These are small hand tools used by railroad Station Agents to safeguard envelopes and packages containing currency or valuable items with wax seals. They were made with either a fancy or plain wood handle attached to a bronze or brass matrix, or they came entirely in one-piece brass or bronze. The matrix had indented letters and numbers stamped in reverse, producing a legible impression in the wax seal. Wax sealers were discontinued shortly after World War II. Those from early now defunct roads have a higher value. All wax sealers listed here are in perfect condition, with their original handles. Those with the matrix badly scratched, nicked or defaced, or with cracked, chipped or replaced handles are discounted in price.

Express companies also used wax sealers, and these parallel those of the railroads, and are also being collected. Wells Fargo Express appears to be the most popular and brings the highest prices in this group. Wax sealers that are dual marked, with both railroad and express company names, are rarities and command top prices.

RAILROAD

"AT&SF RY—Agent, Gage, Okla.," tall iron handle. . 100.00
"AT&SF RY—Agent, Lyons, Kans.," brass toadstool handle
. . . . 85.00
"B&Me RR—Agent, Charlestown, N.H.," wood handle. 95.00
"B&MR RR—In Neb., Nelson," brass toadstool handle150.00
"B&MR RR CO—No. 59," fancy wood handle. 150.00
"CB&Q RR CO—Randolph, Ia.," hollow brass handle. 105.00
"CB&Q RR—Bussey, Iowa," fancy wood handle. 125.00
"C&EI RR—Fountain Creek, Ill.," wood handle. 75.00
"C&G RY CO—Agent, Elizabeth, Miss.," wood handle. 85.00
"CGW RR—142, New Hampton, Ia.," hollow brass handle
. . . . 125.00
"CGW RR—Forest Park, Ill.," wood handle. 95.00
"CM&StP RY—F.S. Div. Fargo," brass toadstool handle
. . . . 75.00
"CM&StP RY—Mitchell Station," wood handle. 85.00
"CM&StP RY. CO—S.M. Div. Fedora," wood handle. . 75.00
"CM&StP RY. CO—S.C. & D. Div. Stickney," wood handle
. . . . 75.00
"CMStP&P RR CO—S.M. Div. Madison, S.Dk.," wood handle
. . . . 75.00
"CRI&P RY—Agent, Banks, Ark." hollow brass handle. 75.00
"C&NW RY—Station, Faulkton," brass toadstool handle
. . . . 100.00*

Railroad wax sealers

"C&NW RY—Agent, Geneva, Neb.," hollow brass handle
. . . . 85.00
"CStPM&O RY CO—Herman, Neb.," brass toadstool handle
. . . . 125.00
"GC&SF RY—Ballinger, Tex.," brass toadstool handle. 95.00
"GF&A RY—Agent, Local, Ala.," brass toadstool handle
. . . . 110.00
"GN RY CO—A-13 Dining Car Dept.," wood handle. . . 95.00
"GREAT NORTHERN RY. CO.—Anoka, Minn.," brass toadstool
handle. 85.00

"GREAT NORTHERN RY—Treasurer," brass toadstool handle
. . . . 100.00
"GTR—Groveton," brass toadstool handle. 75.00
"IC RR CO—Leroy, Ill.," brass toadstool handle. 100.00
"IC RR—Agent, Barnes," fancy wood handle. 95.00
"IC RR—Ticket Office, Hills, Minn.," hollow brass handle
. . . . 100.00
"ILL. SO. RY—Agent, Flat River, Mo.," brass toadstool handle
. . . . 95.00
"KCM&B RR—Sullicent, Alabama," iron bulb handle. 115.00
"KCStJ&CB RR—Amazonia, Mo.," hollow brass handle
. . . . 165.00
"KANSAS CITY SOUTHERN RY—Freight Station, Joplin," wood
handle. 95.00
"L&N RR CO—Agent, K.C. 190, Paris, Ky.," wood handle
. . . . 75.00
"M-K-T RR CO—Agent, Deerfield, Mo.," brass toadstool handle
. . . . 85.00
"M&NW RR CO—New Hampton, Ia.," brass toadstool handle
. . . . 175.00
"M&O RR"—brass toadstool handle. 75.00
"M&StP RY—McGregor, Conductor," large wood bulb handle
. . . . 200.00
"M&StP RY—Algona," wood toadstool handle. 175.00
"MO PAC RY CO—Agent, Chatfield, Ark.," brass toadstool handle
. . . . 75.00
"NEW YORK CENTRAL RR—B 184, Albany, N.Y.," wood
handle. 75.00
"NOR PAC RY CO—Maddock, N.D.," brass toadstool handle
. . . . 85.00
"NOR PAC RR—Anoka," brass toadstool handle. 85.00
"NWP RR—Willits," wood handle. 75.00
"PW&B RR CO—212," pewter toadstool handle. 95.00
"RRI&StL RR—Bushnell," wood handle. 165.00
"SC RR CO—29, Agency," wood bulb handle. 100.00
"SOUTHERN RY CO—Branchville, S.C.," wood bulb handle
. . . . 75.00
"SOU PAC CO—Marshfield, Ore.," wood bulb handle. . 75.00
"TStL&KC RR—144," fancy wood handle. 150.00
"UNION PACIFIC—548," wood handle. 75.00
"WABASH RR CO—37," nickel toadstool handle. 85.00
"WABASH RR—Dining Car Dept.," nickel toadstool handle
. . . . 125.00
"WC RR—Ore Docks, Ashland, Wis.," fancy wood handle
. . . . 135.00
"WIS CEN LINES—Ironwood, Mich.," wood handle. . 125.00
"WStL&P RY—No. 197, Dining Car," brass toadstool handle
. . . . 150.00
"W&StP RR—Redwood Falls Station," hollow brass handle
. . . . 150.00
"Y&MV RR CO—Isola, Miss.," brass toadstool handle
. . . . 115.00

RAILROAD AND EXPRESS DUAL MARKED

"AM.RY.EX.CO., C&NW—Merrill, Iowa," wood handle
. . . . 175.00
"NAT'L.EX.CO., NO.7, C&A RR," wood handle. 200.00

"NOR.PAC.EXP., NP RR CO—Clear Lake, Minn.," hollow brass
handle. 250.00
"RY.EX.AGY.INC., CGW—Clarksville, Iowa," wood handle
. . . . 185.00

TERRITORIAL

"THE A.T.& S.F.RY., Agent, Bartlesville, I.T.," fancy wood handle
. . . . 250.00

"S.C.&D.RR, Sioux Falls, D.T.," fancy wood handle. .250.00

EXPRESS COMPANY

"ADAMS EXPRESS COMPANY—5186, Burlington, Iowa," broad
toadstool handle. 135.00
"AM.EX.CO.—No. 2, Atalissa, Iowa," iron bulb handle. 75.00
"AMERICAN EXPRESS CO—Milroy, Minn.," nickel bulb handle
. . . . 50.00
"AMERICAN RAILWAY EXPRESS CO—Fingal, N.D.," hollow
brass handle. 30.00
"AMERICAN RAILWAY EXPRESS CO—2154, Messenger,"
wood handle. 35.00
"CANADIAN PACIFIC EXPRESS—653," brass toadstool handle
. . . . 125.00
"NATIONAL EXP.CO—Willshire, Ohio," wood bulb handle
. . . . 95.00*
"NOR.PAC.EX.CO—746, Goven, Wash.," brass toadstool handle
. . . . 185.00
"RY.EX.AGY.INC—Public, Hastings, Minn.," wood handle
. . . . 30.00
"SOUTHERN EXPRESS COMPANY—534" wood bulb handle
. . . . 35.00
"SOUTHERN EX.CO.—4797, Whitakers, N.C.," brass toadstool
handle. 55.00
"WELLS FARGO & CO.'S EXPRESS—Hampton, Minn.," wood
bulb handle. 150.00

"WELLS FARGO & CO. EXPRESS—442," iron bulb handle
. . . . 100.00
"WELLS FARGO & CO. EXPRESS—Southard, Okla.," hollow
brass handle. 125.00
"WELLS FARGO & CO. EXPRESS—1758, Messenger," hollow
brass handle. 115.00*

Express Co. wax sealers

WAX SEALING ACCESSORIES (The various torches,
lamps and other implements used in melting the sealing wax,
the sticks of sealing wax themselves and the early money
package envelopes forwarded by railroads and express companies are also being picked up as accesories to the wax sealers.
They are bringing good prices, too.)

SEALING WAX—stick, railroad-marked, old stock, used.3.00
SEALING WAX—box, railroad-marked, new stock, brown, four
sticks, ⅝" square, 10½" long. 15.00
SEALING WAX—box, Express marked, new stock, red, four
sticks, ⅝" square, 10½" long. 10.00

UTENSIL—for melting sealing wax, torch type, height 2½", tin
spout with wick, hook handle. 37.50*
UTENSIL—for melting sealing wax, lamp type, height 2½", brass,
enameled, cap for wick, regular handle. 65.00
UTENSIL—for melting sealing wax, tray type, 3½" x 5½", brass,
complete with alcohol burner and ladle. 85.00*
MONEY PACKAGE ENVELOPE—Express Co., early, original
wax seal impressions on backside (scarce). 25.00*
MONEY PACKAGE ENVELOPE—Railroad, early, original wax
seal impressions on backside (scarce). 40.00
MONEY PACKAGE ENVELOPE—Railroad, pre-WW II, unused
. . . . 5.00

Utensil for melting sealing wax

Early Express covers with wax seals intact

WOOD TOKENS

Wood tokens were made of brass or copper, varying in size from a nickel to a half-dollar. They had the denominations of ¼ to 1 cord wood stamped on them, along with the engine number. Some also had the railroad's initials included on them. In the early days of wood-burning locomotives, these were used by the railroads in payment for cord wood supplied by farmers and others at fueling stops along the railroad's right-of-way. The railroads had money in the home office or on deposit in various banks where they could be redeemed. These tokens are very scarce and carry a premium price.

"M.C.R.R.112"—stamped on obverse, "½ cord" on reverse, brass
. . . . 85.00
"M.C.R.R."—stamped on obverse, "½ cord Eng. 13" on reverse,
  brass 85.00
"M.S. & N.I.R.R.—E & N DIV."—raised on obverse, "¼ cord,
  Eng. 48" on reverse, copper 95.00*
"WOOD-Engine No. 136, ½ cord"—stamped on obverse, reverse
  blank, brass 75.00

Obverse and reverse of brass cordwood token

MISCELLANEOUS THINGS

There will always be miscellaneous things and odds and ends turning up. The question is, "What price will they bring?" Here are a number of them not included in the foregoing categories.

BELL—horse, early street railway, cast brass, raised letters "ST.P. CITY RY. CO." around bottom skirt, 3″ high, 3″ diameter, original iron clapper 150.00
BOTTLE—glass, 1¼″ x 2″ x 5¾″, embossed "Southern Pacific Co. Hospital Department," cork stopper 12.50
BILLFOLD—leather, imprinted with Great Northern Ry. goat logo. Has inside clip just for paper money 12.50
BRAKEMAN'S CLUB—wood, 28″ long, marked "M&StL RY CO." Hartwell Hickory trademark 20.00

BROOM—depot, handle length 38″ with 16″ straw, railroad-marked, "Made by O.K. Broom Co., Chgo." 10.00
BROOM—track, handle length 33″ with 8″ metal tip, 14″ heavy duty straws, "OK Broom Co., Chgo." 12.50
BRUSH—coach seats, "N.Y.C.&H.R.R.R.", 1900s 17.00
BRUSH—clothes, wood w/bristles, oval, "Great Northern Ry." on extended handle, 9″ 35.00*
BULLETIN BOARD—depot, train arrival and departures, wood, black, 30″ x 36″, UP shield logos and name 95.00

Clothes brushes

COAT HANGER—wood, marked "THE PROPERTY OF THE PULLMAN CO.".............................8.00

COLLAPSIBLE DRINKING CUP—aluminum, round, "Great Northern Ry.Co. News Service" embossed on lid....15.00

DEPOT CLOCK—Seth Thomas, wall, eight-day, marked "SOO LINE".......................................325.00

DINING CAR CHIMES—with mallet, "Deagan, Chgo.".50.00

DOOR PLATE—depot, brass, cast SOO LINE logo above doorknob hole, 3½" x 16½", (scarce)............45.00

FEATHER DUSTER—coach, wood handle with turkey feathers, 24" long, railroad-marked.....................25.00

FIRE EXTINGUISHER—glass tube, chemical type, 18" long, embossed "C&NW RY.," cast iron wall brackets......65.00

FLASHLIGHT—Bakelite, two cells, 7" long, incised "AT&SF RY CO."...15.00

LAMPSHADE—ceiling, depot, metal, green enameled outside, white inside, 14" diameter.....................12.50

LAMP—depot platform, pole mounted, kerosene, adjustable self-extinguishing device, "Dietz," early 1900s........300.00

LEAD SEAL PRESS—"RAILWAY EXPRESS AGENCY," cast iron, shaped like pliers, 10" long, imprints number and location on lead disc, used for sealing cloth bags......35.00

LITHOGRAPH PLATE—copper, rectangle, ⅛" x 5" x 7½", w/etched N.P. diesel locomotive.................25.00

MATCH BOX HOLDER—wall type, cast brass, open ends, 1⅛" x 2¼" x 4", mount holes, R.R.-mkd.............65.00*

MATCH STRIKING PLATE—wall type, cast brass, grilled surface, 1¾" x 4½" mount holes, R.R.-mkd........45.00*

POCKET SAVER—for shirt pocket to clip pens and pencils, railroad name imprinted on overhang tab..........3.00

Wall mount matchbox & striker plate

PAINT BRUSH—pure bristle, 2" long, "PRR" monogram on handle, "RUBICO"................................8.00

POKER CHIPS—set of 60 in box, 20 each, blue, red, white, both sides marked with G.N. RY. goat logo...........50.00

POLICE WHISTLE—brass, "B&O RR" incised on top 25.00

POLICE WHISTLE—black plastic, "PRR" monogram inlaid at side.......................................15.00

PRINTER'S TYPESETTING BLOCK—metal die on wood, 1" x 2½" x 2½", Great Northern Railway goat logo...10.00*

PROPERTY PLATE—brass, oval, 1½" x 3½", N.P. RY. (raised) stamped digits and letters, mount holes............8.00*

Printer's typesetting blocks

Brass property plates

RAILROAD SPIKE—narrow gauge road, "Colorado," 4½" long 2.50

RAILROAD SPIKE—standard gauge, 6" long, gold plated, souvenir of steam excursion trip, railroad-marked....5.00

SCALE—counter type, two-sided dial, weighs up to 60 lbs., pan marked "RY. EX. AGY.," cast iron base, 6" wide, 17" long 125.00

SEMAPHORE SIGNAL ARM—metal, original paint, three colored glass lenses, red, yellow, and green, 72" long 175.00

STEEL RAIL—narrow gauge road, "Colorado," cut and polished desk piece, 3" high, 3" long, dated 1882........15.00

SEAL EMBOSSER—cast iron, lion head type, for railroad or express company seals on important papers.......150.00*

STONEWARE JUG—10½" high, 7" diameter, top part brown, "ROCK ISLAND LINES" in blue stenciled on white under glaze in front................................85.00

Embossing seal

THERMOMETER—wall, metal, 2½″ x 10″, "G.N.RY.," indented numerals on brass background, "Taylor".........50.00*

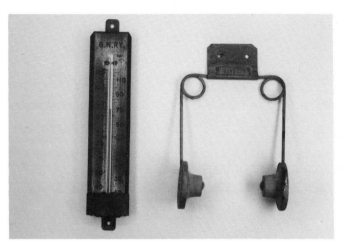

Thermometer and toilet paper holder

STONEWARE JUG—11″ high, 7″ diameter, top part brown, "CHICAGO, ST. PAUL, MINNEAPOLIS AND OMAHA RAILWAY CO." stenciled in blue in front. "Stop Look Now Listen Coal Waste And Oil cost money, Let's save it on this run Please" stenciled on backside.............125.00

STRONG BOX—metal, key locked, hinged lid, 13½″ x 20″ x 11″, original paint, lettered "D.S.S. & A. RY." across front 150.00

TETHER WEIGHT—cast iron, 8″ diameter, 2½″ high, 30 lbs., raised letters around top, "AM. RY. EX. CO." with serial number.....................................150.00

TIMETABLE HOLDER—wall type, metal, 8¾″ x 12″ x 4″ deep, for depot use, railroad-marked in front...........65.00

TOILET PAPER HOLDER—wire frame w/wood roll holder, wall mount plate embossed "CMStP&P RR"..........65.00*

TRAIN ORDER HOOP—bentwood type, with metal clip attachment to hold train orders, 48″ length............37.50

WALLET—leather, black, railroad name and/or logo w/slogan imprinted in silver on frontside. Example: "B&O, Linking 13 States With The Nation".......................15.00

WASTE BASKET—wire grill, pie-plate bottom, 14″...15.00

WHISTLE POST SIGN—cast iron, shield shape, w/big "W" raised inside rolled rim, 16″ x 18″, original paint........75.00

If you'd like to keep yourself current on railroad collectible finds, you should join The Railroadiana Collector's Assn., Inc., P.O. Box 365, St. Ignatius, Montana 59865.

RAILROAD-RELATED COLLECTIBLES

There are objects made in the form of the locomotive, and many items picturing the train, to be found. Although these are not authentic railroadiana items, those who generalize will usually include some of them in their collection. Here is a representative listing:

BANK—locomotive, pot metal, bronze finish, "Railroadman's Federal," ca. 1950s..........................25.00

BIRTHDAY CAKE TRAIN—ceramic, 6 pieces, locomotive, circus cars and caboose........................15.00

BOTTLE—snuff, dark amber, 4½″ tall, "Railroad Mills," train on label...................................30.00

BREAD PLATTER—clear glass, 9″ x 12″, "Fast Mail Train" impressed, ca. 1880s..........................75.00

CALENDAR—Traveler's Insurance, 1885, engraving of train 75.00

CANDY CONTAINER—locomotive, glass with lithographed tin closure depicting cab interior.................25.00

CANDY CONTAINER—locomotive, glass, "999" tin screw cap closure rear..................................45.00

CANDY CONTAINER—railroad lantern, red glass, tin flared base and top, wire handle, 3¾″ high................15.00

CANDY CONTAINER—signal lantern, green glass, tin screw top closure, wire handle, 3½″ high................15.00

CHOCOLATE MOLD—early 6-wheel locomotive, tin, 5″ x 6″ 65.00

COVER—U.S. 1895, has freight train across full length w/ad copy, used 25.00

CRACKER JACK PRIZE—tin locomotive, "No. 512," ca. 1920s 20.00

CRAYONS—"Dixon Railroad," white chalk crayons for marking freight cars, etc., 4″ long sticks, box, one gross....10.00

CUP & SAUCER—old time locomotive and coaches, "England," ca. 1930s................................25.00*

Miscellaneous china depicting trains

DESK ORNAMENT—hopper car, pot metal, on felt padded base, 2″ x 6″, embossed "The Pittsburg & Midway Coal Mining Co., Kansas City, Mo.".............................75.00*

Coal car - desk ornament

DOMINOES—box, "Double Nine," train on cover, engine embossed on dominoes, ca. 1910.................35.00
FLASK—"Lowell Railroad," amber, ½ pint, early 19th century 200.00
GREETING POSTCARD—birthday, toy locomotive, Germany, 1910..15.00
MAGIC LANTERN—glass slide picturing train, Germany 10.00
MATCH SAFE—pewter, early locomotive, embossed both sides 50.00
MIRROR—pocket, advertising, "Traveler's Ins. Co.," picture of passenger train at night......................35.00
MOVIE PLACARD—"Rails Into Laramie," 11″ x 14″, color 10.00*

Railroad movie placards

MUG—china, old-time locomotive and coaches, "B&T" hallmark, England, ca. 1890s..........................65.00
PAPERWEIGHT—medallion type, 3″ dia., bronze, advertising item, "The National Lock Washer Co., Newark, N.J.," passenger train depicted in center, ca. 1920s......35.00
PAPERWEIGHT—steel, locomotive wheel, 4″ dia., w/raised words "Locomotive and Car Wheel Tires".........20.00
PINBACK—celluloid, 1″ dia., advertising "Metro-Goldwyn Pictures," steam train depicted in center, ca. 1930s...10.00
PLATE—china, "Currier & Ives Express Train," Adams, ca. 1930s 75.00
POCKET KNIFE—photo of mallet locomotive, 4¼″ long, ca. 1910...50.00
POCKET KNIFE—"Traveler's Ins. Co.," embossed steam train, 3¼″ long, ca. 1910.........................35.00
POCKET WATCH—Ingram, $1.00 watch, kids, locomotive on dial and back cover, ca. 1930s.................35.00
POSTAGE STAMP—U.S. 1869, regular issue, 3¢, locomotive, mint...................................... 100.00
POSTAGE STAMP—U.S. 1901, Pan American issue, 2¢, passenger train, unused, very fine...............50.00
POSTAGE STAMP—U.S. 1912, Parcel Post issue, 5¢, mail train, unused, very fine..........................35.00
POSTER—movie, "Rock Island Trail," ca. 1950s.....35.00
POSTER—circus, "Ringling Bros., Barnum & Bailey," railroad scene, 26″ x 39″...........................150.00
RAILROAD HERALDS—tin, set of 28, cereal premiums, 1950s 50.00
RAILROAD HERALDS—tin, set of 25 only, 3 missing from original set, re-runs, late 1970s.................15.00
SHAVING BRUSH—old locomotive, England, recent...10.00
SHAVING MUG—occupational, locomotive, ca. 1875.150.00
SHAVING MUG—occupational, baggage car, 1910...125.00
SHAVING MUG—old time locomotive, England, recent.15.00
SIGN—tin, advertising "Pay Car Chewing Tobacco," railroad pay car......................................50.00
SIGN—tin, advertising, "Altoona Beers," Horseshoe Curve and trains, 1950s...................................75.00
SOUVENIR PLATE—china, Germany, hand-painted scene of train on high bridge in North Dakota.............35.00
SPOON—souvenir, sterling, "Altoona, Pa.," train on handle, Horseshoe Curve in bowl, dated 1906...........45.00
STEIN—porcelain, lithopane base, "Corps. of Ry. Const. Engineers," locomotive on pewter lid, Germany, 1884 .... 150.00
STEVENSGRAPH—train, "The Present Time," Great Britain 75.00
STICKPIN—"Travelers Ins. Co., Hartford, Conn." raised locomotive on small gold-plated disc, early 1900s...25.00
TIMETABLE—Airways, associated with the railroads. Example: Northwest Airways, Inc., assoc. with 6 railroads for Air-Rail service, 1931................................15.00
TOBACCO TIN—Fast Mail train on cover, pat. 1878.250.00
TOOTSIETOY—Pennsylvania locomotive 4-6-2 type, 6″ long, pot metal......................................15.00
TRADECARD—"Soapine," model locomotive, 1880s...12.00
TRINKET BOX—locomotive, Staffordshire, ca. 1890s..55.00

Two Important Tools For The
Astute Antique Dealer, Collector and Investor

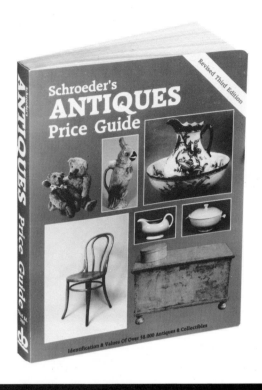

Schroeder's Antiques Price Guide

The very best low cost investment that you can make if you are really serious about antiques and collectibles is a good identification and price guide. We publish and highly recommend **Schroeder's Antiques Price Guide.** Our editors and writers are very careful to seek out and report accurate values each year. We do not simply change the values of the items each year but start anew to bring you an entirely new edition. If there are repeats, they are by chance and not by choice. Each huge edition (it weighs 3 pounds!) has over 56,000 descriptions and current values on 608 - 8½x11 pages. There are hundreds and hundreds of categories and even more illustrations. Each topic is introduced by an interesting discussion that is an education in itself. Again, no dealer, collector or investor can afford not to own this book. It is available from your favorite bookseller or antiques dealer at the low price of $9.95. If you are unable to find this price guide in your area, it's available from Collector Books, P. O. Box 3009, Paducah, KY 42001 at $9.95 plus $1.00 for postage and handling.

Schroeder's INSIDER and Price Update

A monthly newsletter published for the antiques and collectibles marketplace.

The **"INSIDER"**, as our subscribers have fondly dubbed it, is a monthly newsletter published for the antiques and collectibles marketplace. It gives the readers timely information as to trends, price changes, new finds, and market moves both upward and downward. Our writers are made up of a panel of well-known experts in the fields of Glass, Pottery, Dolls, Furniture, Jewelry, Country, Primitives, Oriental and a host of other fields in our huge industry. Our subscribers have that "inside edge" that makes them more profitable. Each month we explore 8-10 subjects that are "in", and close each discussion with a random sampling of current values that are recorded at press time. Thousands of subscribers eagerly await each monthly issue of this timely 16-page newsletter. A sample copy is available for $3.00 postpaid. Subscriptions are $24.00 for 12 months; 24 months for $45.00; 36 months for $65.00, all postpaid. A sturdy 3-ring binder to store your **Insider** is available for $5.00 postpaid. This newsletter contains NO paid advertising and is not available on your newsstand. It may be ordered by sending your check or money order to Collector Books, P. O. Box 3009, Paducah, KY 42001.